A LEGACY LIVED

A LEGACY LIVED

*Your Enduring Influence
for Future Generations*

L. ALLEN MORRIS
— *with* —
BARBARA R. THOMPSON

— *Edited by* —
IDA MORRIS BELL

Editors: Ida Morris Bell and
Barbara H. Thompson
Pathway Communications Group
P.O. Box 1131, Decatur, Georgia   30031

Cover Design: Brad Young, BY Design
543 Sundown Trail
Cassleberry, Florida   32707
bbyoung@compuserve.com

Looking Glass Books
730 Sycamore Street
Decatur, Georgia   30030

Manufactured in the United States of America

ISBN 0-9640852-7-5

To my grandchildren,
to their children and their children,
In the hope that they will find inspiration
from our family story.

——————————

Don't worry about anything; instead,
pray about everything;
tell God your needs and don't forget to
thank him for his answers.

If you do this you will experience God's peace,
which is far more wonderful
than the human mind can understand.
His peace will keep your thoughts and your hearts quiet
and at rest as you trust in Christ Jesus.

Philippians 4:6-7
The Living Bible

PREFACE

"For many years, Allen was a model and a mentor for other Christian businessmen. In today's world, there are far too few 'giants' in business and industry who are also spiritually mature leaders."

Bill Bright, President
Campus Crusade for Christ

It was at the Fontainebleau Hotel on Miami Beach, in the fall of 1960, that I met Allen and Ida Morris, one of the most outstanding couples I have ever known.

I was there to speak at a gathering of executives. My wife, Vonette, and I had just arrived when Allen and Ida introduced themselves to us. Vonette and I experienced an immediate rapport and felt a deep sense of connection with them.

Allen and Ida invited us to their home for dinner and to spend the night. We enjoyed every minute. Later, I learned that Allen was one of the most successful and respected businessmen in Florida.

Some years later, Allen attended one of our Arrowhead Springs Executive Seminars, and we became better acquainted. Shortly afterwards, he was invited to become a member of the board of directors of Campus Crusade for Christ, where he served for over 22 years. I feel fortunate to have such a dedicated, godly board of directors, and Allen, with his wise counsel, was one of the most effective and insightful members.

Allen was such a remarkably astute businessman, yet he possessed a rare ability to balance his material success with his spiritual commitments. He had a great heart for God and played a major role in furthering God's kingdom through Campus Crusade for Christ, his local church and other Christian endeavors.

Together, Allen and Ida built — and Ida continues to build — a godly legacy through their children, their "in-loves," and their grandchildren, all of whom know and love the Lord Jesus. What a legacy! It is one that I am sure will continue for generations yet unborn.

May their tribe increase.

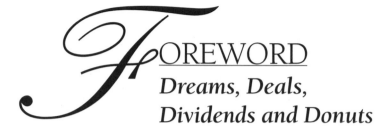

FOREWORD
Dreams, Deals,
Dividends and Donuts

Ida Morris Bell, Kay Morris Rupp and W. Allen Morris

This book is a tribute to the remarkable life of our father, L. Allen Morris, and our mother, Ida Akers Morris, who was the encouraging and modifying force behind our father for more than 50 years.

Daddy played many roles: businessman, Christian and civic leader, hunter and collector, husband, father, grandfather and friend. We sometimes whimsically title these varying aspects of his life Dreams, Deals, Dividends and Donuts.

Dad was a visionary, a creative thinker and an implementer. He saw the possibilities for people, property, projects and problem solving. He also searched out liabilities. Many times

Dreams as we were growing up Dad would dream aloud, expressing far-fetched ideas about things he would like to do or places he would like to visit. A pivotal factor in his success was choosing which dreams to keep as fantasy and which to pursue. Dad had the incredible ability to discern the difference and go for his Best Dreams.

In our family, we had the freedom to dream without being ridiculed or criticized. There was an atmosphere of mutual respect. Over time, we began to realize that we all have dreams, big or small, and that they are a healthy part of the creative spirit that God has given us.

Our dad made deals from the time he was nine years old, when he recruited his friends to sell *Liberty* magazine for him. Then over the years he honed and sharpened his persuasive negotiating skills.

Deals Dad often said, "One of the most important things you can ever do is decide what is the most important thing to do — and then do it." There is a lot of wisdom wrapped up in that simple statement. Dad was gifted at getting straight to the heart of the matter. He could cut through very complicated business discussions and reduce them to simple, effective actions.

You couldn't grow up in the Morris home without hearing talk about investments in property or the stock market, about appreciation (financial, as well as personal expressions of thanks) versus depreciation, and about **Dividends** other complex business terminology. As we grew into adulthood, we discovered that the buildings and properties Dad spent so much time developing had appreciated in value.

Dad also taught us about investing in the stock market, and we discussed several companies that might be good possibilities. He allowed us to make our own decisions, which often cost us money but taught us important lessons, including his Morris truism: If you want reliable dividends, i.e., money in the bank, be conservative and invest in blue-chip stocks.

Another kind of dividend began with relationships. It meant investing personal time and energy in people, whether they were close friends, relatives, or someone in Christian ministry whom we hardly knew or perhaps never had met.

Mother and Dad rarely discussed the importance of doing thoughtful things for others. They just did them. The dividends that still return from their investments in other people's lives are often invisible and usually immeasurable. These are the dividends of eternal significance that God multiplies beyond our wildest imaginings.

Daddy loved to surprise us by coming home with a big box of a dozen, freshly-baked, warm, sugar-glazed Krispy Kreme donuts. They were so good and such a wonderful treat, as we ate them in the kitchen with a glass of milk. Over the years, buying donuts and taking the grandchildren to breakfast on Saturdays or summer mornings brought out the fun-loving, frivolous side of "B.D." ("Big Daddy" — the name Dad is called by the grandchildren).

Donuts

Hospitality also fell under the category of donuts, at least in our family. Mother and Dad always loved to entertain at home, whether in Coral Gables, Atlanta, or Black Mountain. When we were children, we learned how to prepare the house for "company." Mother did most of the cooking and flower arranging herself.

Dad and Mother had that special gift of "Southern hospitality" — making people feel welcome and comfortable in their home. We say Southern hospitality because they obviously learned it from their families, growing up in Atlanta. Regardless of what some might say, there is a particular quality of graciousness and charm, love and caring, that is still pervasive in much of the South today. When you add the dimension of the love of Christ, it is quite amazing.

Despite all the good stories you will read in this book, we aren't a perfect family and Daddy never claimed to be a perfect father or businessman. We all have our irritating habits and personality quirks. Often we stumble and fall; sometimes we even get up with mud on our faces. But we keep on forgiving each other when tempers flare, when patience runs thin, when we run late and keep others waiting. We continue to struggle toward honesty with each other, listening to criticism, striving to grow and change while seeking God's direction for our lives.

Our hope and heart's desire is that, through this book, the lessons and examples Daddy offered can indeed serve as an enduring influence for future generations.

Let this be written for a future generation,
that a people not yet created may praise the Lord.
Psalm 102:18

ONTENTS

CHAPTER ONE
Birth of a Salesman

I still remember that day. It was an unusually warm day in Atlanta, in December 1923. I was nine years old, and my friends and I were playing in an empty lot. None of us seemed to notice the automobile which stopped at the curb.

"Hey, kid!" A well-dressed man yelled from the window of his car, motioning me to come over. "Want to make some money?"

I hesitated for a moment. "Doin' what?" I didn't know why he had singled me out; maybe he noticed that I was taller and more mature looking than the others.

"I'm the district manager for *Liberty Magazine*," the man explained. "I'm looking for energetic boys to sell 10 magazines each week to their neighbors and make 25 cents for a couple hours work."

He waited a moment and then asked, "Think you could do that?"

"Well, I guess so." What boy wouldn't accept an offer like that? Twenty-five cents was a lot of money in 1923.

The magazine man suggested I get approval from my mother. Our home was only a few doors away, and when he explained the opportunity, my mother agreed to let me try my hand at salesmanship for a while. I was elated!

The manager told me that he would bring 10 magazines on

the Wednesday following Christmas. I was to sell them for five cents each, keeping two and a half cents for myself and paying the manager the rest.

I sold my first copy of Liberty Magazine the next week. I can still see the cover — it had an attractive, 1924 calendar printed in color. In those days, calendars weren't as available as they are today, and it was easy to sell the first 10 magazines.

Expanding Markets

Within an hour, I returned home with 50 cents in my pocket. Half of it, 25 cents, was mine to keep. It was more money than I ever dreamed I could make in such a short time.

My desire to make more money compelled me to work harder. I began selling farther from my home, until finally I was selling 30 to 40 magazines every Wednesday after school.

The manager suggested that I ask some friends to work for me. If I could sell as many as 50 copies, I could buy them for one and a half cents each. If my friends sold 10 magazines apiece, I would make one cent on each copy they sold.

Soon I was receiving more than 100 magazines every Wednesday. That, as it turns out, was only the beginning.

Once I had covered my neighborhood, I decided to head to downtown Atlanta, where hundreds of people worked every day. I rode the streetcar for seven cents. Mustering up my courage, I began with the Healy Building on Broad Street and asked the building manager for permission to sell magazines there. He agreed. As long as I didn't bother the tenants, I could walk by the desk of each employee on Thursday and ask them if they would like to purchase a Liberty Magazine.

I had the distributor leave a package of 50 magazines in the barbershop on the ground floor of the building. As soon as school ended, I picked up the magazines and took the elevator to the 16th floor. Then I walked back down, covering every floor. In fact, I usually sold all of the magazines before reaching the first floor. After a while, people working in the Healy Building expected me and genuinely looked forward to getting their copy of the magazine.

I thought, "If I can do this at the Healy Building, why not at the 12-story Palmer Building?" Mr. Palmer, a real estate developer, gave me permission to sell my magazines at his historic building at 101 Marietta Street.

The Palmer Building had large floors and was full of Southern Railway employees working on rate books and tariffs. It had a high-density population (at that time, I was unaware of how important this is). In retrospect, I am surprised that I was allowed to sell magazines at both the Healy and the Palmer buildings, because they were two of the largest and most important buildings in Atlanta.

By that time, I was working after school on Thursdays in the Healy Building, on Fridays in the Palmer Building, and on Saturdays in my own neighborhood. I had six boys selling magazines for me, each in his own area, and I ordered nearly 200 magazines every week.

> *I learned early on that you don't get anywhere without sharing your part of the burden, and if you do more than your share, you get rewarded. I also learned to make every minute count. These were lessons that I would draw on for many years to come.*

With six boys selling 15 magazines apiece, I made 90 cents. At the same time, I sold 100 magazines myself, with a profit of three and a half cents per magazine. For two to three afternoons of work a week, I was making $4.40. (In 1924, if you made 10 cents an hour, that was pretty good money. I'm not sure that a day laborer made even a dollar a day.)

When I was younger, my parents had given me an allowance of 35 cents a week. Now I paid my own living expenses and never asked them for any money. Of course, back then you could buy a hot dog and a Coca-Cola for five cents each!

As an incentive to get boys to sell more magazines, the company issued a green coupon for every five magazines sold. Ten green coupons could be redeemed for one brown coupon; several brown coupons could be redeemed for wonderful prizes.

I remember earning a football, a new baseball glove and roller skates. I also saved enough coupons to get a fountain pen for my father. But my happiest moment came when, after saving several hundred brown coupons, I gave my sister, Katherine, a new Ranger bicycle for her birthday.

Soon I was recognized as the top salesman for *Liberty Magazine* in Georgia. Looking back on this experience of selling magazines as a boy, I realize that it started me in business. I genuinely liked people, and I loved selling.

THE WORLD IN
1914

It was a pivotal year, a time that transformed forever the political and cultural landscape of the world. Europe plunged into the nightmare of its first "total war." Within four years, 10 million were dead and 17 million wounded. Vladimir Lenin and the Bolsheviks had seized power in Russia, and the sun was setting on the British Empire. Meanwhile, the United States emerged as a world power. In 1918, at the war's end, a mysterious flu virus encircled the globe, killing another 40 million people in Europe, Asia, and America.

Against this somber background, extraordinary advances were made in science. Robert Goddard began experimenting with rockets, and Albert Einstein proposed his General Theory of Relativity. Max Planck developed the quantum theory and won the Nobel Prize for Physics. An English scientist, Baron Ernest Rutherford, split the atom, and Dr. Alexander Graham Bell made the first transcontinental telephone call.

In the arts, D. W. Griffith released the movie *Birth of a Nation*. Jazz swept the United States, and George M. Cohan wrote the song "Over There." In sports, Bobby Jones made his debut as a golfer, and the managers of the New York Giants and the Cincinnati Reds were arrested for playing the first baseball game on Sunday.

CHAPTER TWO
Roots and Wings:
An Atlanta Childhood

I grew up at 460 Candler Street, in the section of Atlanta known as Inman Park. When my father and mother were married, he bought this house, I am told, for $2,000. It was here I was born, on January 7, 1914.

As a young boy, I learned a great deal about life and relationships from my mother and father and from my grandparents and great-grandparents.

Both my mother and my father grew up in families that had been committed to the church throughout the generations. My paternal great-great-grandfather, John Morris, founded the Cedar Grove Church of Conley, Georgia. The original church was a log chapel built in 1828 and dedicated as "Morris Church" in the Methodist denomination.

A Heritage of Faith

Three of John's sons, including my great-grandfather, George Washington "Watt" Morris, became Methodist ministers. John's friends jokingly accused him of building a church so that his sons could have pulpits!

The History of Cedar Grove Methodist Church speaks highly of "Watt" Morris' abilities in the pulpit:

> It has been said that Uncle Watt, in his preaching days, spoke with such ease and fluency that one was reminded of string rolling off a ball. He lived to the age of 93, long after the church was moved to its present site. The aged minister asked to be buried so that his head would be placed on the spot where the pulpit of the old church stood. This was done.

I spent most of my early summers with my mother's family in Gordon County visiting her grandparents, John and Cloey Camp. John Camp was in his seventies, and he was the justice of the peace, the postmaster, and the owner of the general store and blacksmith shop. He was a tall, commanding, robust man with white hair and a full white beard. During the Civil War, he had served as a captain in the militia, and his blacksmith shop was a small armory where rifles were made for Confederate soldiers. Later he gave land and helped build the West Union Baptist Church, where he taught the men's Bible class and was one of the original deacons. People called him "Deacon" or "Old Squire Camp." My great-grandmother also served the church, baking unleavened bread for each communion and providing California port wine.

A history of the Camp family records some of the stories my great-grandparents would tell us about the Civil War:

> When J. L. Camp came home from the war, he found his house burned and all his livestock gone. His wife and small daughter were still living in the smoke house. He saw what a terrible welcome the returning soldiers were getting. Confederate money was not good, and the state of Georgia was bankrupt.
>
> John Camp had buried several thousand dollars in gold before he went to war. He promised all the veterans he knew that they could come with him, and he would furnish food and shelter and pay when he could. Ten vets came: a gunsmith-blacksmith, a furniture maker, a brick mason and

seven willing men with their families.

They put Rocky Creek on the map in twenty years. They built West Union Baptist Church and maybe fifty houses within ten miles of the church. They also built a lumber mill, a general store with post office, lodge room and offices, and a flour mill with the newest machinery. J.L. Camp built a school house and furnished it with desks and teachers at his own expense, and it was free for all children.

John Lumpkin Camp and Cloey Robinette Camp were married for 63 years, until his death in 1921. They had four daughters.

One of those daughters was my grandmother, Emma Adelia Camp Calbeck. She and my grandfather, Orlando Calbeck, also had a house at Rocky Creek, with a large pasture and peach orchard. Their other neighbors were the Marion Fuller family. The sons, Cecil and M.F., were about my age, and we used to play and work together all summer long. I got up at daylight to help them with their chores, watering the stock, and milking in the morning and afternoon. When M.F. and I were old enough (around age 9), we began driving the cultivator as well.

When we first arrived for the summer, before our own well was cleaned out, my job was to go to the Fuller's and get buckets of water. Everyone went barefoot in the summer. Before my feet got tough, it was terrible to step on the rocky road between our houses, especially when I was loaded down with two big buckets of water.

A Simpler Life

My grandparents' house had a tin roof and was not winterized. Whenever it rained, there was a horrible racket. The windows were open all the time, and all the outdoor noises came in. As children we heard frightening stories about things happening at night, and it was nice to be upstairs in our bedroom, safely under the covers.

It was extremely quiet in the country, and there were still a lot of people using a horse and wagon. A few people owned Model-T Fords. In fact, it was so quiet, we could hear one coming a mile away. We could even identify the car's owner just from the sound.

Whenever a storm damaged the road, the men took their shovels and picks and repaired it. Keeping the road open was a community effort.

No one had electricity then; we used kerosene lamps at night and cooked on a wood-burning stove. (Every single bite of food was absolutely delicious; no one had to make you eat!) There was also no running water. We had one telephone line, and whenever anyone received a phone call, all the phones in the community rang. Everyone knew everyone else's business.

Our refrigerator was a shelter built over the well. On one side of the shelter was a series of shelves. On the top shelf, my parents put a large pan filled with water. They covered it with a cloth, which dropped toward the ground. The cloth absorbed the water from the pan, and as the water ran down the cloth, it evaporated and lowered the temperature on the shelves. This is where we stored our milk and butter and watermelons.

We attended church every Sunday morning. Sometimes, late Sunday afternoon, the church had a "singing." The families gathered on the church grounds for fellowship before they returned home to tend chores — milking the cows and feeding the livestock. One of the highlights of the sing was homemade ice cream, which some of the ladies brought for refreshments.

Memories of a Country Church

The Baptist church met on the first and third Sundays of each month, with the preachers coming by horse or buggy. On alternate Sundays, the Methodist church held their services. Whenever the preacher came, it was an all-day affair: people brought fried chicken, biscuits and other good things to eat for lunch. We would stand around under the huge, shady oak, talking and catching up on the news of the day. About four o'clock, it was time for the homemade ice cream that people had been churning in their freezers.

At age nine, I went with a friend to Johnson Chapel, a little country church where a Methodist circuit rider preached. On that summer Sunday, the preacher spoke about Jesus dying for our sins, and how much He wanted us to believe in Him. I felt that I saw Christ right there.

After his sermon, the preacher asked people to come forward and give their lives to Christ. I stood up and went forward. Even at that young age, I knew that if Christ had died for my sins and wanted me to be loyal to him, I wanted to

An Early Conversion

do just that.

Afterwards, the preacher baptized me with water from a peanut butter jar. All of this created quite a bit of gossip in the valley: Old Squire Camp, a devout Baptist, had a grandson who joined the Methodist Church!

My father was an extrovert, and it seemed that he liked everyone, and everyone liked him. My mother was more of an introvert and often seemed deep in her thoughts. She was proper and conventional, and rarely showed any emotions, unless something really important to her became disappointing. Looking back, I believe I adopted many of my mother's more inward traits, while at the same time, becoming an extrovert like my father. Above all, my family was devout and religious.

My family went to Druid Hills Methodist Church, it seemed, all the time. My father was a steward and Sunday School teacher; my mother was involved in the women's work. Church was our social life, because there was too much work to do during the week to leave time for other activities.

In the early twenties, the highlight of my summer was the Children's Day picnic on the grounds of the Cedar Grove Church. My father was famous for his Brunswick stew; my uncles, for their barbecue. When people asked my father about his ingredients, he always gave the same answer, "One cow, one pig, one squirrel, one rabbit, and several other things I'd rather not tell you about!" My favorite foods were the delicious cakes my aunts would bake.

My father, whose nickname was "Jack," had an outgoing personality and made friends easily. Toward the end of his life he was often ill, but he always had a smile on his face.

As the southeastern representative of The Spool Cotton Company, a subsidiary of Coats & Clark's, my father sold and distributed thread. He opened up the whole Southeast for the company. Because his territory was so large, he traveled a lot and usually was home only on weekends.

Honesty and ethics were very important to my father. He had

a great appreciation for his family, and he made it clear that part of my responsibility in life was to protect my mother and my sister. He was always complimentary toward me and gave me a great deal of self-confidence.

Because of his failing health, my father retired from The Spool Cotton Company in 1933. He then went to work selling life insurance. After a long illness, he died on January 9, 1936.

My mother attended Shorter College in Rome, Georgia. After graduation, she taught school in Calhoun. Like my father, she could see the humor in situations, and she had a gift for hospitality. She was not a gossip, and she never talked about anyone in an unkind manner. She also was not a complainer. She taught me not to display feelings of disappointment or discouragement.

". . .May God forbid that we should have anything but joys, but dear, I realize that we will need to have our dark days to make us appreciate bright ones. The adage is a true one. Every sweet has its bitter, and it is a poor rule that does not work both ways."

--Excerpt from a letter written by my father to my mother two years before they married

She often told of her feisty grandmother's encounter with Sherman's troops when they came through Rocky Creek and her grandfather was away at the war. Only the women were at home, and the soldiers took all the food and livestock, then went under the house to see if my grandfather was hiding there. My grandmother told the soldier, "He's no Yankee dog; he wouldn't be hiding under the house!"

My mother wasn't the kind of person who told me not to do things. She just said, "I'd rather you wouldn't do that."

That's what she said one day when I asked her if I could go swimming at the public pool on Ponce de Leon Avenue in Atlanta. I went anyway. I was in the middle of the pool, when some bigger boys sunk my raft. I went down three times before the lifeguard got to me. When I woke up, they were giving me artificial respiration by the side of the pool.

After that, if my mother said that she'd rather I didn't do something, I didn't do it!

During those years, communication with the world outside Atlanta was limited. Telephones were not as common as they are today, and our telephone number was "44J." Atlanta had two newspapers, but there was no regular radio news. (I remember building my first crystal set about 1924. It was a simple procedure: I wrapped copper wire around a quart ice cream container, connected the crystal, tuned in a station, and heard President Calvin Coolidge speak that same day!)

I grew up thinking that people in New York knew more than we did in the South, simply because they were better informed. As a pre-teen, I was inspired by the out-of-town businessmen who visited my dad from their home offices in New York. I liked the way they dressed, their air of sophistication, and their optimistic outlook on the future.

> **My parents taught me to love the Lord, to be absolutely honest, to respect other people, and to do the things I said I was going to do.**

My father often invited his friends over to hear the latest news from these visiting executives. After a delicious meal of my mother's fried chicken and other Southern specialties, everyone would retire to the living room. The local men asked questions about business conditions and practices in New York, and the women were interested in fashions on Fifth and Park Avenues.

I noticed that my father's friends seemed to have an uncanny respect for the New Yorkers and their business acumen. They hung on every word the visitors said.

From those gatherings, even at my young age, I realized that knowledge was important to success. The more you knew, the more people listened to you and believed what you had to say. I decided then to be an avid reader, to try to be a good listener and a fair conversationalist. I also decided to move to New York, when I finished school, and work for a New York company.

THE WORLD IN
1928

Delegates from 65 nations, including the United States, met in Paris to outlaw war with the signing of the Kellogg-Briand Pact. Germany began to regain some of its pre-war prosperity. One seldom heard the name of Hitler, except in jokes, and the National Socialist Party (Nazi) had only 108,000 members. In the Soviet Union, Joseph Stalin implemented a "Five-Year Plan" to collectivize agriculture and transform the USSR into a model of economic development.

In the United States, a decade of prosperity was heading toward its last, optimistic hour. Republican Herbert Hoover predicted "the final triumph over poverty" and won a landslide victory over his Democratic opponent. Average income was $750 a year, and one in four Americans were invested in the bull stock market. Economists applauded "the permanence of prosperity."

It was a year for extraordinary advances in medicine, including Alexander Fleming's discovery of penicillin. Amelia Earhart became the first woman to fly as a passenger across the Atlantic, and George Gershwin wrote "An American in Paris." Talking movie pictures were one year old. The first cartoon with a soundtrack, *Steamboat Willie*, showcased the talents of a new film star: Mickey Mouse.

CHAPTER THREE
Boy's High: Grocer, Boy Scout, Sailor and Student

By the time I started high school at Boys' High of Atlanta (now Henry Grady High School), I was six feet one and weighed 165 pounds. I began feeling that working as a "magazine boy" was a little below my dignity, so I got a job at the A&P supermarket. I worked at two different stores — first at the Atlanta Curb Market on Edgewood Avenue and then at the Moreland Avenue store at Little Five Points.

My weekly pay was $3.50 for working Friday afternoon and then all day Saturday, from 6 a.m. to midnight. It was less than I made selling magazines, but I believed that now I was in the real business world.

Deli Psychology

I tried to soak up all the knowledge I could about the retail market. When we graded eggs, separating them by size, I noticed we could sell the larger eggs for 14 cents a dozen, while still selling the small ones for 12 cents. Even separating the brown eggs from the white pleased some customers; they were willing to pay 16 cents a dozen for the large white eggs.

It was my job to keep the produce counters clean and supplied, while cutting cheese and taking groceries to customers' cars.

The cheese was on a hoop shaped like an automobile tire, and I became adept at cutting just the right amount. I learned never to cut too much: it was better to add a little than to subtract from a customer's order. Customers were cost conscious and did not want to pay for more than they ordered. The same was true when I was scooping sugar or candy.

> *The customer felt like he was getting a full measure if I started small and added on.*

Saturdays were especially long and tiring. After working 18 hours, carrying 100-pound bags of potatoes from the back room, as well as numerous other packages and crates of canned goods, I would get home after midnight. Yet without fail, I always got up early Sunday morning to go to Sunday school and church with my family. I was also a member of the Epworth League, our Methodist youth group that met on Sunday evenings. Aside from work and church, there wasn't much time for sports or extracurricular activities.

One outside activity that was very important to me was the Boy Scouts. I joined when I was 12 years old. About a year later, my father and I were out hunting, and he asked me how I was progressing. I told him I was a second-class Scout, because I hadn't taken the test to be first class.

"Anything worth doing, is worth doing well," he told me. "If you don't like Scouts well enough to progress in it, do something else. If you like it, then progress as rapidly as you can."

Toe to Toe with Jack Dempsey

As a result, I became a first-class Scout, and then, in 1929, an Eagle Scout. I earned 22 merit badges, and they all required a great deal of work.

I received my Eagle Scout badge from Jack Dempsey, who was the world heavyweight boxing champion. The ceremony was held at the Atlanta Athletic Club on my 16th birthday. Because I was over six feet tall, I didn't have to look up to too many people. However, I remember that as I walked toward Jack Dempsey, he kept getting bigger and bigger. By the time I shook his hand, he was huge!

During my sophomore year at Boys' High, I joined the Reserve Officers' Training Corps (ROTC) to earn extra money. I was paid nine dollars a month to drill and attend a training class once a week.

When I was 16, as part of the training program, we took a cruise to the Caribbean on the *USS Taylor*, an old World War I destroyer. We learned how to do everything from polishing brasswork and launching emergency lifeboats to shooting the five-inch guns.

Caribbean Cruise, Navy-Style

During gunnery practice, each person had a special assignment. The gunnery officer on the bridge determined the distance to the target and phoned the information down to the guns. For example, if the target was 1200 feet away, the chief gunner's mate turned a calibrator on the gun so that the shell would not hit the water for 1200 feet.

Two people were needed to sight the gun: one for the up-and-down motion of the ship and one for its forward motion. When the command was given to fire, we had three seconds to get the shot off and two seconds to put in a new round. We were graded on how long it took us to fire five rounds. We were supposed to be able to load, fire and reload five times in 25 seconds; we thought we were pretty good if we could get our time down to 23 seconds.

On my first cruise, two older sailors accused me of stealing a wallet they claimed they had left on a table in the crew's quarters. They said that if I didn't give them "the money," they would report me to the commanding officer, and I would be court-martialed. It was a scary situation!

The men knew that I was young and sailing on my first cruise. I didn't know what to do, so I went to my commanding officer and told him that they had accused me. I'm sure that was the last thing those older men expected me to do, but it turned out to be the right decision. That was the end of it.

From this experience I developed a lifelong appreciation for the problems of enlisted men, and I was a better officer in World War II, because I understood from firsthand experience the situation of young people in the Navy.

As children and teenagers, we would get together in a group

on Sunday night — that was the nearest thing we had to dating. My mother held an open house for my sister every Sunday night, and my friends as well as my sister's friends were always welcome. Mother was such a warm and friendly hostess that even many years later, when I met old friends in my travels, they would ask how she was getting along.

I learned a great deal from the actions of these men, including that you can't take everyone at face value. There are people out there who, instead of looking out for young people, try to browbeat them and take advantage of them.

The Great Depression was a terrible experience for almost everyone. There were people selling pencils and apples on the street, and you could get a dozen eggs or a quart of milk for 12 cents. A loaf of bread was five cents, and pork "side meat" (streaks of fat and lean) was four cents a pound.

During the Depression, people fried all the fat out of the side meat. Then they mixed flour and salt and pepper into the liquid fat. They gradually added milk, stirring constantly to make "chicken" gravy. It was absolutely delicious when served as a substitute for meat on toast or biscuits.

One night I went over to a friend's house for dinner. His mother served steaks that we had to cut with a knife! At our house, we had not eaten meat that had to be cut for as long as I could remember. Usually our "ground round" steak was made into a stew or cooked as hamburger.

Depression Cuisine

During the Depression, many things happened around me that were a terrible shock. I had a friend who lived across the street. One night his father came home from a disappointing day of job hunting, went out in the backyard and shot himself. The father had a wife and children to support, and he had been looking for work for weeks. He simply could not find a job.

I overheard adults speculating that the man thought his insurance money would pay the mortgage on his house and provide his family with some money to survive the Depression. I realized then that a father's first thought ought to be to provide for his family, and this awareness made a lasting impres-

Dark Days

sion on me.

During the Depression, there were so many men like this neighbor who could not find jobs. Seeing their desperation gave me an even stronger desire to earn money.

Part of my father's job was to drive throughout Georgia and introduce thread products to stores that served people living in small towns. It was a hard task for a person in poor health, because traveling on country roads was difficult.

Most of the country roads in Georgia then were rocky and unpaved. Just driving from Atlanta to Calhoun (a 60-mile trip), you could count on having one or two punctures. Tires were primitive, and if you had a flat, you had to get out, take the wheel off, and repair the puncture before continuing on your journey.

When it rained, the red clay roads were slippery. It was easy to slide into a ditch if you had to pass a car coming from the opposite

Primitive Tires, Slippery Roads

direction. Usually, you had to walk to the nearest farmhouse and find a farmer and a team of mules to pull you out.

When I was old enough to drive, I sometimes went with my father on his trips. He would let me drive, and I also helped repair the tires.

During those years, to make matters worse, my father suffered from an acute stomach disorder and high blood pressure. He was attended by a leading group of doctors in Atlanta, but none of them was able to find a cure. The medicine they gave him for his stomach caused his blood pressure to rise to dangerous levels, and his blood pressure medicine increased his stomach problems. As a result, he had constant headaches and chronic stomach pain. (A gastroenterologist recently told me that today my father would have lived in comfort, with the medicines that are now available for his blood pressure and stomach upsets.)

My father's physical problems became progressively worse, and from 1930 on, he was sick most of the time. This, of course, caused my family great concern and uncertainty.

As my father's health deteriorated, our meager savings dwindled. One day, in 1932, when I graduated from Boys' High, my father called me in for a conference. As he had done many times before, he told me how important it was to go to college. He said that he would have preferred to have a more responsible position with his company in their New York office, but this door was closed to him, because he did not have a college degree. It was the one thing he wanted for me more than anything else.

A Father's Struggle

Then my father took a $100 bill from his wallet. He said, "Son, this is all I can give you for your college education," and handed me the money. "But you are always welcome to live at home," he added. "And we will always have a room and food for you."

For the first time, I realized that I wouldn't be going to Duke University in Durham, North Carolina, which had been my dream for many years. I learned that my only choice was to live at home and attend Georgia Tech. I was disappointed, but in the years ahead, this decision proved to be a fortunate one. In my travels throughout the world, when people learned that I had gone to Georgia Tech, they responded knowingly. Many quoted from our fight song: "I'm a Ramblin' Wreck from Georgia Tech, and a helluva engineer!"

I was determined to get a college degree, and with $100 in hand, I began checking out the cost of tuition at various schools.

THE WORLD IN
1932

The Great Depression had spread around the world. In the United States, 12 million workers were unemployed and over five thousand banks had closed. Once prosperous businessmen begged on street corners, and the popular song, "Buddy, Can You Spare a Dime," captured the desperation of millions of the newly poor.

Americans responded to the crisis by turning to new leadership. Democratic candidate Franklin Roosevelt soundly defeated Republican incumbent Herbert Hoover and ushered in a "New Deal" with a series of "fireside chats."

Meanwhile two English scientists smashed the atom, and Werner Heisenberg was awarded the Nobel Prize for the development of quantum mechanics. Shirley Temple starred in her first film, and the entire nation was shocked by the kidnapping and murder of the baby son of Charles and Anne Morrow Lindbergh.

HAPTER FOUR
College and Courting

Registration day, 1932. I handed the Georgia Tech registrar my $100 bill to pay for my first semester, my student fees and my books. She handed me back $33, all I had left to pursue my education and get the degree my father cherished for me.

I still remember the orientation talk on the first day of chapel in September. The Dean said, "I want you to look at the person on your right and then at the person on your left. At the end of six weeks, one of you three will not be here."

These were frightening words. I asked myself if it would be I who flunked out. "No," I decided. "I'm going to study, and I'm going to graduate." The Dean had awakened a competitive spirit that has stayed with me to this day.

Commerce to Textiles

I began my studies majoring in commerce, a general business course that included accounting, typing and advertising. Advertising was almost a course in psychology. We also learned design, layout, and production. I enjoyed production (which included selecting and using different typefaces) because I could visualize exactly how I wanted the finished product to look. Then it was just a matter of getting it done.

In my freshman year, Governor Eugene Talmadge pressured the State Board of Regents to transfer the commerce school at Georgia Tech to the University of Georgia. The Governor was an alumnus of the University, and most people believed that he was trying to provide an easier course of study for the athletes there. The more exacting engineering and math courses stayed at Tech.

In 1928, Georgia Tech's football team was number one in the nation. After the Board of Regents moved the commerce school to Athens, it was many years before Tech was able to regain its reputation as a leader in college athletics.

Because of this move, I had to reconsider my major. After talking with my father, I switched to textile engineering. Textiles seemed to be the future of the South.

Georgia Tech was one of the best things that ever happened to me. I was immersed in experiences that prepared me for both life and my career. I quickly learned how to make good use of my time. There was never a minute when I could just sit around and shoot the breeze

As freshmen we had to speak to everyone on campus. It was excellent training, and I met a lot of people whom I would not have known otherwise.

with friends. I was either studying or working, or participating in extra-curricular activities.

I took my course work extremely seriously. Every day, at the end of classes, I came home and set up a card table in the living room, and did my homework. When I was finished, I folded up the table and put it back in its proper place.

It was a ritual that I carried out for all four years of college.

I first met Ida Akers when I was on a double-date — with another girl. Ida was extremely attractive and personable, and I

Right Date, Wrong Seat

was immediately impressed. We were in my car, and I was driving, but all my thoughts were with Ida!

Ida was a junior at Washington Seminary (a private girls' school, now Westminster School), and we started dating soon after our double-date. I wasn't in love yet, I just liked her. Occasionally I invited her to dances at Tech. Ida was so popular, that I had to ask her a month in advance to get a date.

In those days, the orchestra played four "no breaks" and two "specials," when the songs were slow and sentimental. On all the other songs, any one could break in at any time on a dancing couple.

When Ida and I were dancing, there always seemed to be a line of guys just waiting to break in on us. I would get in about four steps, and then it was someone else's turn. All the girls had a card on which they wrote their "no break" and "special" partners. I always tried to get at least one of each on Ida's card.

Because of my heavy schedule, most of my social life was limited to Saturday and Sunday nights. Ida's mother, like most mothers of the girls I knew, had an open house for boys on Sunday. I would drop by to listen to records, eat snacks and talk. There were always a lot of other young men with the same idea.

No one seemed to have a surplus of money for dating in those days. A big event was a trip to the Varsity, a popular drive-in restaurant. For 25 cents, you could buy two hot dogs and two Cokes and leave a five-cent tip.

The summer after my freshman year, I worked at the Coats & Clark's Thread Mill in Austell, Georgia. I made $8.15 a week, for 12 hours of work, five days a week. My room was at a boarding house run by a mill supervisor, and his wife cooked three big, delicious meals a day. I still recall that wonderful southern food! I paid $5 a week for room and board and saved $3 for my college expenses.

Through conversations with the mill's general manager, William R. Beldon, I soon learned that mill work wasn't for me. Beldon had spent his entire life preparing for his top management position in the mill, which included supervision of the mill village, where the families of the mill workers lived. Yet he told me that he earned only $5,000 a year. This

A Road Not Taken

was a lot of money during the Great Depression, but I thought he deserved much more for his experience and responsibility.

Because of my summer job experience, when I returned to Georgia Tech in the fall, I changed my major to industrial manage-

Letters Home, 1933
Coats & Clark's Thread Mill, Austell, Georgia

June 23, 1933

There was quite a bit of excitement last night, when one section on the night shift threatened to strike for higher wages. It was about ten o'clock, and Mr. Beldon was there at the time. He, the sly old fox, promised a raise of 25% within the next two weeks. Said he was glad they did it, and that he thought they were satisfied at the present wage scale.

The innocents went back to work, not realizing that their hours also would be shortened in the next two weeks, and that they would be making less than they are at present. For instance: at 25 cents an hour (few workers make that), a man makes $13.75 for a 55-hour week. A raise of 25% (which is .31 1/4 per hour), with a 40-hour week, means only $12.50 a week. Not bad thinking on Mr. Beldon's part, huh?

July 5, 1933

I certainly do miss you all. I believe it is better for me not to come up so often, as I miss you more if I see you. The leaving part is the hardest.

I see that the next textile law has been passed and will go into effect on Monday. That certainly is fine, and I sure am glad that I won't have to work so long . . . . One of the girls, who runs a comber, caught her hand in the machine and tore one of her fingers off. I don't know how she could have done it.

ment. I spent one more summer working in Austell. A federal law had been passed limiting the work week to 48 hours and raising the minimum weekly wage to $14.40. This was thirty cents an hour, almost double the previous hourly rate.

After making the honor roll in my freshman year, I was allowed to work in the science lab, filling beakers for 40 cents an hour. My wages came from the Federal Education Assistance Act. On weekends, I worked at the stadium during football games and, when there were no games, at the A&P grocery store.

On Saturday nights, I sponsored dances at the Biltmore Hotel. I rented the ballroom, hired an orchestra for half the ticket sales (excluding the hall rental), and then sold tickets for fifty cents. As it turned out, we always had a full house.

Georgia Tech's student newspaper was called *The Technique*, and because I loved to write, I joined the staff as a freshman. It seemed easy to find interesting stories from students and faculty, and to cover sporting events and other college happenings.

At that time, Georgia Tech did not have a public relations department, so I also worked as a student reporter for *The Atlanta Journal*. Whenever something of news value happened on campus, I submitted a story to the paper. I was paid 50 cents a column inch, so I put "who, what, when, why and where" in the first paragraph, and then enlarged on that as much as I could!

> *I gave football players and other athletes free tickets, because I knew if they came, so would everyone else.*

At the end of my junior year, I was elected editor of *The Technique*. It was a position I had worked for since my freshman year, and I felt honored to be chosen for the job. Culver Kidd of Milledgeville, who later became a leading Georgia politician, was my astute business manager.

The paper was run entirely by students. Because of this, the editor and business manager were responsible not only for writing and publishing but for distribution and advertising (to pay for printing and overhead). At the end of the year, if there were any profits left over, the editor and the business manager divided them equally.

With this in mind, every week I challenged Culver to get more and more advertising. Much to my delight, at the end of our senior year, we had made a profit of $2,400. I paid the remainder of my college expenses with my share and still had $1,000 left.

At that time, Georgia Tech had a rifle team. In my senior year, I was elected co-captain, and we won the national collegiate championship. William Randolph Hearst gave a heavy gold medal to each member of the team, and to this day, our plaque hangs in the Georgia Tech Naval Armory.

I was also a member of the Reserve Officer's Training Corps. As a freshman, I was given the option of joining either the Army or the Navy. I thought about long days and nights in all kinds of weather, eating hard tack (unleavened bread used as army rations), so I chose the Navy. I wasn't crazy about water or the ocean, but at least in the Navy I would be warm, with plenty of food . . . or dead.

In 1933, because of his poor health, my father retired from the Coats & Clark's Company. It was a terrible time for him when he realized he couldn't travel anymore. He had worked for Coats & Clark's for 32 years, and the people he sold thread to had become good friends.

When my father retired, the company gave him an annuity policy, which was an unusual step at that time. It paid him $79 a month. During those Depression years, this was a lot of money, especially if you owned your house.

After his retirement, my father went to work selling life insurance for "Woodmen Of The World." Today people have money and realize they need insurance, but during those years, it was very hard to sell life insurance.

Watching my father work so hard for so little, I felt great despair and love for him. He was fighting a battle he couldn't win, and I felt closer to him than I had ever felt before.

By the end of 1935, my father was extremely ill. His medicine no longer controlled his blood pressure, and he was admitted to St. Joseph's

Remembering My Father

Hospital in Atlanta. The doctors told us that he would not be going home again. My mother spent every day at the hospital, and she was exhausted from the long vigil. I began to worry about her health as well.

My father died on January 9, 1936. It was two days after my 22nd birthday, and five months before I received the college degree he wanted so badly for me. He was only 55 when he died, leaving us a legacy of love and high standards. If he had lived today, with our superior medicine for controlling blood pressure, it is unlikely that he would have died so young.

In the thirties, there were few young men with any college training and even fewer with college degrees. As a result, a lot of large corporations came to Georgia Tech seeking new employees. These companies were giving preference to graduates with a lot of extra-curricular activities. I considered myself fortunate, because I had plenty!

At graduation, I was offered eight jobs in corporate training programs. Two were in New York. The first was with the Vick Chemical Company, which promised to pay me $125 a month, with a $25 living allowance when in New York. The second was from Coats & Clark's, which offered to pay me $250 a month.

Despite the smaller paycheck, I chose the job with the Vick Chemical Company. I was impressed with their training program and thought I would learn more with them than with Coats & Clark's. I also wondered if Coats & Clark's had offered me the job because of my father, and I wanted to make it on my own.

Each year Vick Chemical Company interviewed the top two or three students at colleges and universities across the country. Then, based on grades and extra-curricular activities, they chose 20 young men to participate in their training program. I felt privileged to be one of those 20 trainees.

Endings and Beginnings

My mother had sacrificed for me, and loved and encouraged me throughout my college years. After graduation, I decided to use my left-over newspaper earnings to buy her a graduation gift. I visited several car dealerships in downtown Atlanta and finally chose a new, steel-grey Ford. It was a V-8 sedan with a radio and heater — all the accessories available in 1936. The best deal I found was in Calhoun, Georgia, and I paid $825 for that beautiful new car.

My mother had decided to move to Los Angeles, where her mother and brother lived, so that my sister could attend the University of Southern California. The summer that I graduated I drove them both out to California and said goodbye. I wasn't worried about my mother starting over in a new community. She was a strong, intelligent woman, and I knew she could make a place for herself.

In California, I boarded the USS Chaumont for my first tour of duty as an ensign in the Naval Reserve. I served as officer of the deck. The ship sailed down the coast of California, through the Panama Canal and terminated its voyage in Norfolk, Virginia.

It was 1936, and I was 22 years old. I had $175 in my pocket, and I was heading North to work in the city of my childhood dreams: New York!

THE WORLD IN
1936

For the second time in the twentieth century, the world stood at the brink of war. German troops marched into the Rhineland at the French border, an area which had been declared a demilitarized zone at the Versailles Treaty ending World War I. Civil war erupted in Spain. Mussolini and Hitler formed the Rome-Berlin Axis, and Joseph Stalin continued his purge of the Communist party, killing more than a million members.

In the United States, Franklin Roosevelt was elected to a second term in another landslide victory. Margaret Mitchell sold a million copies of her new book, *Gone with the Wind*, and Dale Carnegie wrote *How to Win Friends and Influence People*. Meanwhile, in Berlin, black American track star Jesse Owens won four Olympic gold medals, dashing Hitler's hopes of turning the Olympic Games into a celebration of Aryan supremacy.

CHAPTER FIVE
Young Man in Manhattan

As I headed to New York, the Great Depression was seven years old, and President Roosevelt was nearing the end of his first term in the White House. In four years, he had made sweeping changes in the government, and his New Deal seemed to be helping the economy towards recovery.

I arrived in New York with a sense of expectation and optimism for my future. Vick's training program lasted for three months, and included instruction in marketing, manufacturing, sales and administration. The twenty of us selected for the program were all competitive people, and we all wanted to do our best.

One day, as part of our training, a psychologist walked us around the block, asking us to take a look at various store windows. When we returned to the office, he asked us to write down everything we had seen in the Walgreen's window.

"You need to remember what you see."
— Vick's trainer

Later, he asked to see me. He pointed out that my list was inadequate, and that I needed to improve my powers of observation. It was great advice, and since that day, I have made a point of remembering what I observe. It was one of the most important lessons I learned at Vick.

As a result of this training and numerous aptitude tests, some members of our group went to secretarial school. They were later assigned as secretaries to executives to continue their training. I was assigned to the sales force.

It was then that I put my "advertising training" to good use. Equipped with a Ford panel truck, a folding ladder, assorted signs and a Bostitch hammer that dispensed its own staples, I was sent back South. My area covered Tennessee, Virginia and West Virginia; my job was to travel from town to town, on dusty country roads, nailing up Vick signs on barns and in other conspicuous places. I was also to sell Vick's products to general stores and drugstores.

In those days, the psychology of advertising precluded saying derogatory things about another product. You simply assumed there was no other product. Today, many advertisers compare products and run down their competitors. The goal is to highlight how poor the competition is. Personally, I don't like to buy from a company that claims a named product is poorer than theirs.

We didn't pay farmers to put a sign on their barn; instead, I had to convince them that it was a good idea. I usually explained that our large signs helped seal cracks and keep the hay dry. I also offered them an assortment of Vick's products.

One day, in a general store, the owner gave me permission to put up a sign. I put up one and then another. I was tacking up my fourth sign, when he realized how many I had installed and came after me with a hammer. Needless to say, I quickly exited his store.

On the first sales call I ever made, I was so frightened that my hand wouldn't push down the handle of the door. I had to walk around the block again, to get up the nerve to go inside and give my canned sales talk.

The company wanted us to use a canned sales talk that described the products (Vapo-Rub, Vicks Cough Drops, Vatronol, etc.), how they worked, and why they would bring relief to the store's customers. Unfortunately, this talk didn't sell a thing. As salesmen, we learned to develop our own sales pitch to get orders.

Whenever I went to a town, I called on all the stores that could sell cough drops, including service stations. After reminding them how good Vick's products were, I gave them a choice between a large and medium-sized deal. I never let them know that we offered any "little" deals.

Usually they would take the smaller, medium-sized deal, just because they wanted to buy something from me. I ended up selling Vick's products in just about every store I called on.

I saved the drugstores for evenings, because they were usually open until 9 p.m., and at that hour of the night, the druggists were usually bored. They were sitting around, waiting for someone to call in a prescription, so they would listen to my sales talk. I could make two or three calls like these a night after supper.

My daily routine was simple. I'd hang up signs and sell to general stores and service stations during the day. Then I went to my hotel, took a shower and had a good dinner. (We were allowed 35 cents for breakfast and lunch, and 70 cents for dinner. This included a nickel tip for breakfast and lunch, and a ten cent tip for dinner.) At night, I visited drugstores. It wasn't long before I had the best sales record of any one in the company.

I quickly learned that if I wanted four people to show up in the morning, I needed to get a firm commitment from eight the night before.

It was lonely in those small towns on weekends, especially in the coal mining regions of West Virginia. Fortunately, I had a copy of *Gone with the Wind*, and I read it in poor light in country hotels over a period of three months.

In January, 1937, Vick sent me to Schenectady, New York, to give out product samples. To keep costs down, I recruited my help from bars and saloons.

I paid the men in cash to go door to door, handing out samples. While they walked down each side of a residential street, I walked down the middle, supervising. It was bitter cold, but we did this for several days, until we covered the whole town. By then, I think everyone in Schenectady had received a sample of Vicks Cough Drops, Vapo-Rub and nose drops.

In February, I was sent to Miami. The druggists in Miami were busy looking after tourists and did not want to talk with me.

One day the Vick sales manager, Charlie Lipscomb, came to Miami and spent the day with me. He insisted that I give the standard sales talk. We made ten calls, I gave the same talk ten times, and we didn't sell a thing.

When I pointed out that the sales talk didn't work, Charlie said, "We want you to give the talk to educate the druggist. When someone comes in looking for a cold remedy, we want them to think of Vick's." I could see his point, but I was more interested in selling the customer than educating him.

After six months on the road, Charlie Lipscomb called me back to the home office to be his assistant. He wanted more time

Marketing Cough Drops: "Next to Heaven"

to focus on sales promotion. By then, I had lost my enthusiasm for lunches of soda crackers with cheese, peanut butter or sardines, washed down with warm Coca-Cola (since most rural stores had ice only on weekends). I was glad to get back to New York.

After one week of training, Charlie gave me a private office, a secretary and the key to the main office. I burned the midnight oil and handled the job of assistant sales manager with very little supervision.

In a few months, I rotated out of that job to another part of the training program. This time I was assistant to the manager of the cough drops division. This job was "next to heaven," because I worked with top professionals in the world of advertising.

One of my bosses, Jerry Patterson, was convinced that the three-inch ad for Carter's Little Liver Pills was one of the best ever written. He challenged me to accomplish the same thing for Vicks Cough Drops.

I spent two weeks trying to write this ad, and I must have written a hundred pages of copy. Every time I took a new idea into Jerry, he wadded it up and threw it in the trash basket. I never did succeed in writing that ad, but I did learn to write short copy. And by the time I got through, no one knew more about Vicks Cough Drops than I.

The most important thing I learned was that Vicks Cough Drops were "medicated" and sold for ten cents, while our competitors' cough drops (Luden, Smith Brothers, etc.) sold for five cents. It probably didn't cost us any more than it did them to produce, package and ship the product.

We designed a counter display-box for 24 packages that took up minimal space. The store could put cough drops right by the cash register, so people could see them while they were paying their checks.

The druggist made four and a half cents profit when he sold a package of Vicks Cough Drops but only two cents when he sold another brand. By the late 1930s, we were selling one million packages of cough drops a week. This was a tremendous marketing accomplishment.

One day, while trying to sell Vick's products in New York, I called on thirteen drugstores, and at every store, the manager or clerk was rude and profane. They didn't want anything to do with a salesman.

On my thirteenth call, I had taken all I could stand. I was so mad that I didn't care if I was fired. When the manager was rude, I gave every bit of it back to him, telling him what I thought of him and all the rest of the druggists. He bought my best assorted deal.

I'll never forget the conversation I had one night with some other trainees. We were sitting around talking about how little money we made. Ben Lee, who had a master's degree in chemical engineering, said he would sign a life contract with Vick if they promised him $5,000 every year.

In 1936, that didn't seem like such a bad idea. Our trainee salary was $1,500 a year, and $5,000 seemed like a lot of money. We all had heard a rumor that Jerry Patterson paid $5,000 a year to rent his apartment on Park Avenue, and we thought that was unbelievable.

Later, when I was promoted to sales manager, I made a little more money but had less free time. I worked most nights, as well as Saturdays and Sundays.

I had enough sense to realize that Ida would never live in New York, and that's when I decided I didn't want to live there either. I had fulfilled the resolution I made when I was 12 years old, to spend two years working in New York. Now it was time to go home.

Delivery Lessons

Ida's father, William Akers, was the executive vice president of Haverty Furniture Company in Atlanta. Because of my experience in New York, he offered me a job working in the company's advertising department.

There was an ulterior motive behind my interest. "You know I want to marry your daughter," I told Mr. Akers.

"You will never marry my daughter," he replied. "You don't want to marry Ida. She's spoiled and doesn't know what she wants to do. It'll be a long time before she makes up her mind."

I wasn't deterred; the most important objective in my life was to marry Ida. I accepted the job at Haverty's and, in January, 1939, I moved to Atlanta to be near her.

Mr. Akers did not cooperate. He convinced Haverty's to send me to Little Rock, Arkansas, where I worked in the refinishing department. Later I worked in the delivery department, so that I could learn what types of people bought what kind of furniture.

In delivery, I learned that most of the expensive furniture went to people who could not afford to buy it. We often had to repossess furniture simply because the families were not able to make payments. This really bothered me.

> *I felt that we had a responsibility not to sell people furniture they could not afford, especially if they were not even able to discern that the cost was beyond their budget.*

After an eternity of three months in Little Rock, I was sent to New Orleans to handle advertising in their Haverty's store. Finally, after three months, I was transferred back to headquarters in Atlanta. Here I worked as advertising manager, preparing sales promotions and advertising campaigns (including copy and layout) for all twenty stores. We even developed a marketing program for Simmons "Beauty Rest" mattresses. For five cents down and 35 cents a week, you could "get a good night's sleep for a nickel."

> *"I'd rather have you for a father-in-law than a boss," I said. "I don't want to work for my father-in-law, and I don't think you want me to work for you as your son-in-law."*

During this year, I dated Ida only once or twice a week. Finally, after seven years of waiting, on New Year's Eve, 1939, I asked her to marry me. She said, "Yes."

When her mother and father returned from the Orange Bowl Game in Miami, I officially asked Mr. Akers for permission to marry his daughter. He gave his approval and blessing with as few words as possible.

The next morning, I went into Mr. Akers' office and told him I had decided that it would be best for me to leave Haverty's and start my own business. He said, "One reason I said you could marry Ida was because you had such a good job!"

I admired everything about Ida's father. He was one of Atlanta's leading citizens, an elder at North Avenue Presbyterian Church, a generous contributor to missions, and a successful and honest businessman. I wanted to love him as a father-in-law, especially since I still suffered the void from my own father's death, just three years earlier. I also knew that if I worked for myself, I would be judged on my production, not on my relationship with Mr. Akers.

Ida Akers: A Legacy of Success

"I'm not worried about making a living," I said. "If I can marry Ida, I can do anything!"

Ida was born in Atlanta in 1917, and the first house she lived in was on Inman Circle in Ansley Park. Her father started out in the lumber business and became an investment banker, before

Home Sweet Home

from *The Wall Street Journal*
October 19, 1982

George E. King was a frugal man. Even as a millionaire, he saved string. He was a temperate man, too. "I have loved the taste and smell and the effect of whiskey but have never been a drinker," he once said. "I always have wanted to gamble but have never bet a penny."

But in 1890, when Mr. King built a house for his family, he showed neither stint nor restraint. The home at 889 Edgewood Ave. was a Victorian showpiece, with a grand tower on one end and a broad porch topped with a circular copper canopy on the other. The interior walls were paneled in oak; sunlight glowed through stained glass images of flowers and trees; and carved lions roared from the fireplaces. . . .

It was 100 years ago that George King stepped off the train in Atlanta, a young man with a bowler hat, walrus mustache and soft eyes. He had a reed-thin frame and was about to lose another 30 pounds as he launched his own hardware business in downtown Atlanta. "Adversity makes a good man better," he intoned, knuckling down to 16 hours of work a day. Apparently it did; by 1890, sales at King Hardware Co. had climbed to $125,000 a year. Mr. King raised his annual salary to $2,000 from $1,500 and turned his attention to building a home for himself, his wife, and their eight children.

. . . "That house was made for children," recalls Mary Hart, one of Mr. King's daughters. ". . . There were secret hiding places everywhere," she adds, recalling that she once got stuck between two plaster walls while sliding down the laundry chute.

going to work for Haverty's Furniture Company. Her mother directed the affairs of the Akers household and was a gracious hostess, golfer, civic worker and gardener.

Ida's maternal grandfather, George E. King, was the founder of King Hardware in Atlanta. He was a serious, austere man who in his later years walked to work every day, from 1145 Peachtree (today, the heart of Midtown) to downtown Atlanta. A 1982 article in *The Wall Street Journal* featuring Mr. King is excerpted on

Sayings of George E. King

I have never had a hundred dollars without planning one hundred places to use it or knowing one hundred people who need that particular hundred dollars.

Adversity makes a good man better. Prosperity often destroys the weak.

Ability counts more than location.

We should not only help the worthy, but help also those whose only claim on us is that they need it. Help those who need you, not just those whom you might need.

The whole course of a man's life is determined by his choice of the banner under which he fights. Under what banner are you fighting?

the previous page, and several of the sayings by which he lived — and which have influenced me — also appear above.

As a child, Ida wanted to be a missionary. One year for Christmas, she asked for riding boots, but when she tried them on, they didn't fit. She told her parents if they took the boots back, she would like to give the money to missionaries. They did as she asked. Her father, in fact, took a huge step further. He bought a station wagon and gave it to missionaries.

A Young Heart for Missions

The Akers family always sat on the front row at North Avenue Presbyterian Church. Ida listened carefully, but she never understood what the minister was talking about. She thought, "If I live to be 85, then I'll probably understand this!"

One Sunday, when her brother Billy and she were in high school, they went to hear Peter Marshall preach at his church on Ponce de Leon, Westminster Presbyterian Church. They slipped out of their church and hoped their parents wouldn't notice, since they didn't sit with them.

It was the first time that Ida ever had heard a sermon that she really understood. She was so excited. But her parents noticed that they weren't in church, and they were upset. Ida tried to get them to come hear Peter Marshall, but they said they didn't want to hear any more about it. You just didn't visit other churches back then. Still, Ida went back several times.

Ida and I began our life together on February 28, 1940. We spent our honeymoon in Miami Beach and Havana.

When we returned to Atlanta by train on Saturday night, I had $7.50 left from our savings — and no job. Fortunately, we had already paid two weeks rent on our apartment, which we had rented for $75 a month.

With more than four years experience in national and regional advertising, I felt ready to begin my own advertising agency in the growing metropolis of Atlanta. On Monday morning, I went to C&S Bank and explained my business plan to Mr. Lawrence Gellerstadt, the loan officer. A short time later, I walked out with a loan for $1,500 to finance start-up costs for The Allen Morris Advertising Agency. It was March, 1940, and I agreed to pay the bank back at $50 a month, with 6% interest.

I rented a small office in the Volunteer Building on Broad Street from Robert E. Martin, a friend and respected advertising executive. He was paying only $80 a month rent, and I used half his space for $40. I paid an additional $40 to share the services of his secretary/receptionist.

As a result, my overhead for my new business was $80 a month plus telephone expenses.

I could sell better at lunch than at any other time, because people were more relaxed and under less pressure.

Since I had a monthly loan payment of $50, I knew I had to make at least $130 a month. On top of that, I also needed something to live on and to support my new wife.

Every morning, I arrived at the office early and wrote letters to people I knew, letting them know I was in the advertising business. Then, up until noon, I called on potential clients. I knew many of the business executives in Atlanta, because I had met them when I volunteered with the Red Cross and the Community Chest while working for Haverty's.

When I started my business, I couldn't afford to take people out to lunch. Later, lunch appointments became the key to my sales success. I quickly learned that if you give people something good to eat, they feel happy. When they feel happy, they are more likely to buy your services. (Years later, it was at lunch that I obtained the money to build my first office building.)

If I sold something in the morning, I returned to my office in the afternoon to work out the ideas on paper. Every afternoon, a free-lance artist stopped by to see if I had any new illustrations or presentations for him to do.

After dinner, I worked nearly every night until two or three in the morning, keeping the company's books and writing plans for clients. During this time, I discovered that I was most creative after midnight, when I could get things done without distractions. Ida recalls those early days and the long hours in her own words:

> I learned early in our marriage that I was not going to see much of my husband. Allen had been trained to work all his life, and he was a hard, hard worker. In fact, it's always been difficult for him to relax, and I don't think he could live without working hard at something.
>
> During our first year of marriage, I would write thank you notes for our wedding gifts while Allen worked until one or two in the morning. One night we drove by an office building around 11:00 p.m., and he said, "Look at all those people working so late!" It didn't seem to occur to him that he worked that late every night.

A lot of my business came from referrals. One of my first accounts was the advertising promotion for the Southeastern World Fair, which was actually a state fair. Along with several smaller accounts, I also landed the Irvingdale Dairy.

We introduced a contest to name the "Irvingdale Cow" and ended up awarding a high school girl the prize. Her entry — "Minnie Quarts." After the contest, "Minnie" sent out a monthly publication from Irvingdale with news of the farm, horoscopes and trivia. Milk sales shot up.

I worked closely with my landlord, Bob Martin, and after a few months, we merged our accounts. We changed the name of our agency to Martin & Morris.

As Martin & Morris, we wrote, directed and produced a large number of animated radio spots. Before long we were offered a new serial program for the radio, "The Lone Ranger." Later, we bought "The Green Hornet."

Economy Auto Stores sponsored "The Lone Ranger" every night at 6 p.m. The timing was perfect: it was early enough for children and late enough for fathers coming home from work. Everyone in Atlanta seemed to be listening to this

The Lone Ranger: Riding the Airwaves

program, and soon sales for the Economy Auto Stores soared. Martin & Morris sponsored more commercials on radio station WGST than any other agency.

In the first three months of operation, the agency lost money. By the fourth month, we broke even. Once we crossed that milestone, I never made less than $600 a month. These were not bad earnings in 1940. However, I worked hard: it was not unusual for me to work 18 hours a day, six days a week. On some weekends, I also served in the Naval Reserve, to keep my commission active and to earn some extra money.

Even in these early days, Ida was always helpful and considerate. We couldn't afford to eat out on a regular basis, but once a week I took her out to dinner and to see a movie. That was our recreation.

Breaking Even, Setting Patterns

As the agency grew, so did our savings account, although it was still small by today's standards. Before the end of the year, Ida and I were able to make a down-payment on a $7,000, newly constructed FHA house on Benjamin Harrison Drive.

This time in our lives was wonderful — we even had a dog. On Saturdays, I cut the grass and helped Ida do whatever she needed to get done around the house. We had love, friendship and a great relationship. What we didn't know was that our happy life together was soon to be interrupted by war.

THE WORLD IN
1941

By April, Hitler controlled all of Western Europe, with the exception of Spain and Portugal. Only Britain and the Soviet Union still held against the Nazi-Fascist Axis, and in June, Hitler invaded Russia. Within days, German troops were halfway to Moscow.

In September, Japan signed a formal alliance with Germany and Fascist-Italy, and began implementing a plan to create a new empire in the Pacific. On December 7, 1941, Japanese planes bombed Pearl Harbor, destroying the United States' entire Pacific fleet. On the same day, the Japanese attacked the Philippines, destroying most of the United States air force and forcing General Douglas MacArthur to retreat.

On December 8, the U.S. Congress met in an emergency session to declare war on Japan. Three days later, to the immense relief of Great Britain and occupied Western Europe, Hitler and Mussolini declared war on the United States.

CHAPTER SIX
World War II:
War in Africa

In January 1941, I learned that if I volunteered for my "year of service" in the Navy, I would be discharged in a year. If I didn't volunteer, I was subject to call-up at any time.

Ida and I were expecting our first child in July of that year. Because I did not want to be away from home for months after the birth of our baby, I volunteered immediately. I was glad I had earned my commission as a naval officer while at Georgia Tech.

In February, Ida and I reported for duty in Charleston, South Carolina. My Navy pay totalled $189 a month, a substantial reduction from my income from the advertising agency.

Our first apartment was in the backyard "slave quarters" of Governor Maybank. Maybank, who later became a United States senator, had converted his two-story stables into several small rooms, including a living room, kitchen, den and powder room. Upstairs, there were two bedrooms and a bath. We paid $32 a month in rent and bought an ice box and an old beat up stove, both for $5.

In Charleston, I was assigned to a sub-chaser, a small, fast ship equipped with 50-millimeter machine guns and six to eight depth charges. Every morning, we sailed out at 0800 to look for enemy submarines that might be spying on ship movement in the harbor.

If we sighted a sub, or the bubbles where one had been, we were to report it by radio. If the sub were to submerge, we were to drop depth charges on it. I don't know what we would have done if the submarine had just decided to shoot at us. We never did see a German sub, but there was an atmosphere of alertness and apprehension on the boat that made the war seem close to home.

Looking for Enemy Bubbles

One night, when we returned to our dock at the inshore patrol base, the commanding officer sent for me. "The Admiral wants to see you at 0800 in the morning," he said. Nothing else. I wondered what I had done wrong, but apparently the commander didn't know, because he gave me no clues. Since I was new to active duty, I had no idea what to expect. I had never even seen an admiral.

On the way back to our rental apartment, I stopped by the barber shop. I wanted to look my best for the next morning, and I spent the evening checking out my uniform and polishing my shoes, so that I could look ship-shape when I reported to the Admiral's office at 0750.

Admiral's Aide

Admiral William Allen, Commander of the Sixth Naval District in Charleston Navy Yard, came into his office at 0755. At exactly 0800, his aide told me to go in.

The Admiral asked me a battery of personal questions. "Where were you born? How long have you lived in Atlanta? Who were your parents and grandparents? How long did they live in Georgia?" My answers seemed to satisfy him that my family was deeply rooted in America, with no hint of allegiance to any other country.

As I was trying to figure out why the Admiral had singled me out to ask these questions, I heard him say, "How would you like to be my aide?"

"I'd like that very much, Sir!"

"Turn over your command and report tomorrow morning," the Admiral ordered. "And get your hair cut!"

The next morning, after my second hair cut in 24 hours, I

went to work for Admiral Allen. His behavior was exactly what I expected from a U.S. Navy admiral. He was direct in his conversation and always in command of the situation. Originally from Florence, South Carolina, he was a gentleman in every respect.

Change of Command

Admiral Allen reached retirement age shortly after the Japanese attack on Pearl Harbor and asked to be released from active duty. While I was waiting for his replacement to arrive, I wrote a letter to the Chief of Staff, requesting a transfer to the USS Atlanta. It was a light cruiser being commissioned for service in the Pacific.

The Chief of Staff denied my request. He said, "You'll stay here until the new vice admiral, William Glassford, arrives from the Pacific. Unless he has someone else in mind, he may want you to be his aide."

Admiral Glassford came straight from the war in the Pacific, and all of his clothes and personal gear had gone down with his flagship, the USS Houston. It was sunk by the Japanese in the Battle of Makassar Straits. As a result, when he arrived in Charleston, he had only a couple changes of clothing.

May I Borrow Your Uniform?

I was six feet one and weighed 170 pounds, and luckily for me, the Admiral was the same size. My dress uniforms fit the Admiral exactly; the only difference was the insignia. The availability of my uniforms just might have been what tipped the scales in my favor — the Admiral asked me to be his aide.

The Atlanta Constitution told the folks back home about the missing uniform, writing, "Later, when the sunken gear had been replaced, Admiral Glassford said he was considering taking his aide's uniform for keeps. 'After all, it fits better than these new ones I ordered,' he said, pointing to trousers a bit too long."

I saw the war as an opportunity to develop personally and to expand my knowledge and abilities. With this in mind, I counted myself very fortunate to be on Admiral Glassford's staff. He wouldn't read a single document until I had read it first, even if it arrived "Top Secret, Top Urgent." (I could read those documents *very* quickly!) Admiral Glassford wanted me to know everything he knew, so that I could screen documents and decide what he did and did not need to read.

The Admiral also took me everywhere he went, and because he served as a personal representative to President Roosevelt, with the rank of minister, we went a lot of places. During the course of the war, I met the President and most of his Cabinet. I also met many of the top admirals and generals in the United States, as well as those fighting for the British and the Free French, (including General Charles de Gaulle).

It amazed me that these top commanders treated me as an equal, although I never acted as if I thought we were equals. I assumed that an aide was to be "seen and not heard" unless called upon.

I stayed with Admiral Glassford for the duration of the war (1942-1945). We were together in the Atlantic, the Mediterranean, and the African and European theaters of war. Our ports of call included London, Italy, France, Oran, Algiers, Morocco, Ghana and many other African countries.

Ida and I always tried to be especially nice to the single men who lived in the Bachelor Officers' Quarters and had no family in Charleston. We knew they were lonely, so we often invited them over to our house for a meal or to play bridge.

One of our visitors was Lieutenant Jack Kennedy (later, President John Fitzgerald Kennedy), who came by to play bridge fairly frequently. We became good friends, and I remember him as a charming and friendly young man.

Lieutenant Kennedy had just returned from the Pacific and was glad to be on dry land.

In December, 1942, the Admiral and I received top secret orders to go to Africa. We left out of Miami, but we couldn't tell anyone where we were going. It was a sad parting from Ida and Little Ida on that December day.

In Miami, we met the six other members of our secret mission to French West Africa. Together, we boarded the Coronado, a huge, four-engine transport sea plane (the first to be delivered to the Navy) and headed for San Juan. Then we flew on to Trinidad and Belem, Brazil, where our accommodations were hospital rooms.

Secret Orders

The next day we flew to Natal, on the coast of Brazil, and that evening we made the first-ever, non-stop flight between South America and the continent of Africa. We left at dusk and sighted the African coast at daybreak. The seaplane landed in the harbor of Dakar, the capital and seaport city of French West Africa (now Senegal).

In French West Africa, Admiral Glassford would be serving as deputy to the Commander of the Allied Forces, General Dwight D. Eisenhower. Eisenhower's headquarters were in Algiers, North Africa, where he was fighting one of Germany's most brilliant and successful generals, Erwin Rommel, "The Desert Fox."

Eisenhower needed more light bombers in North Africa as soon as possible. Our job in Dakar was to negotiate with Boisson to enlarge the airfield, with assistance from U.S. Army engineers, and to arrange for U.S. bombers to refuel in Dakar before making the long flight across the Sahara Desert to Algiers.

We successfully negotiated with the local officials to open the Dakar airport to U.S. bombers, to refuel on their way to North Africa. In exchange, we arranged for economic experts from the State Department to negotiate a trade agreement with French West Africa. The U.S. Army Engineers also expanded and improved the airport to handle the new traffic requirements.

By then the country had been under a blockade by the Free French for several years, and there was a shortage of almost all Western goods, including medical supplies. The only food available was raised locally (it included an abundant supply of fish and seafood). In exchange for the country's large supply of peanut oil, the State Department shipped in clothes, fabrics and other essentials that they so desperately needed.

After a few months in Dakar, we returned to the United States to report firsthand on the success of our mission to President

Roosevelt. Ida met me in Washington, D.C. and we had some happy days together in the Jefferson Apartments. I was surprised and pleased to receive a letter of commendation from the Secretary of the Navy for my service as Secretary of the American Mission.

Admiral Glassford was a born diplomat, and I learned a great deal by watching him at work. He seemed to know how to handle every situation. He was

> *The admiral said, "The reason I noticed your lack of confidence is because I didn't have any in myself." I thought that was an amazing admission for an admiral to make to a lieutenant.*

always thoroughly prepared and knew precisely what his objectives were.

One time he told me that he noticed I didn't have a lot of confidence in a plan on which he was working. I was surprised, because I thought I always demonstrated full confidence in him.

Early in January, 1943, a select group of Washington news reporters was informed that President Roosevelt would be making an important trip "somewhere out of the country." For the sake of the President's personal safety, no news about the trip was made public until after his return.

On January 24, 1943, Franklin Roosevelt, Winston Churchill and Charles de Gaulle met in secret with their staffs in Casablanca, the seaport city in northwest Morocco. "It was," said Winston Churchill, "the end of the beginning."

Casablanca: "The End of the Beginning"

For the first time since 1939, the Allies had reason to feel optimistic. American soldiers had defeated the Japanese in Guadalcanal, after one of the toughest military battles in American history. Thanks to British general Bernard Montgomery, the "Desert Fox" was on the run in North Africa. In the Soviet Union, the road to Moscow had become a bitterly cold graveyard for hundreds of thousands of retreating German soldiers.

In Casablanca, Roosevelt, Churchill and de Gaulle mapped

out their strategy for ending the war. They agreed to invade Sicily and Italy, to prepare for a major offensive in the Pacific, and to conclude the war only with the unconditional surrender of Italy, Germany and Japan.

Franklin D. Roosevelt will go down in history as one of the greatest world leaders of all time. However, my opinion of him had been poisoned early on by both my father and father-in-law. They were lifetime Democrats but couldn't accept his statement that "no one ought to make over $25,000 a year." Everyone I knew thought it unbelievable that Roosevelt wanted to limit earnings in the United States, the world's leader in free enterprise.

Listening to these discussions, I never dreamed that one day I would have the responsibility for the President's safekeeping. He would fly into Dakar and then cross the city to the harbor, to board a French destroyer. The destroyer would then rendez-vous with the battleship USS Iowa, while it was anchored in the Dakar harbor.

> *In January 1943, it was my job to secure the safe conduct of President Roosevelt as he returned from the Casablanca Conference.*

We were not allowed to tell anyone that the President was coming. When I asked French Admiral Collinet for a destroyer on a certain date, I had to say to him, "But I can't tell you what it's for." I couldn't speak French, but he agreed. I then asked French General Barreau if his men would guard the road from the airport to the harbor. He also agreed.

Admiral Glassford and I were in Algiers in early January, and we flew to Casablanca before the conference on a B-17 bomber. This plane was assigned to the President's son, Colonel Eliott Roosevelt. The Admiral and Colonel Roosevelt spoke together at length, but the Admiral couldn't tell Colonel Roosevelt why he was going to Casablanca. The security was so tight that no one was allowed to discuss the conference or who would be there. So Colonel Roosevelt had no idea that he was about to see his father.

Neither did my family know the nature of my work, but the

following letter indicates how much they supported me, sometimes without knowing.

> Dearest Mother,
>
> The package filled with all the trinkets and jewelry arrived this afternoon, and I was amazed to see what good quality costume jewelry you had bought . . . . I only wish that you could be here to see the expressions on the faces of the natives when I hand them out.
>
> I am going to give a couple of rings to our wash women . . . who wear a multitude of clothes despite the hot weather. Their names, believe it or not, are Beautiful and Delicious. The real sight is to see them walking up the main street with the family wash precariously balanced on their heads and each arm extended to hold the white uniforms, which they carry on coat hangers . . .
>
> Love to all from your loving son,
> Allen

Then came the dispatches from Casablanca, which always referred to President Roosevelt as "Mr. Jones." One read, "Mr. Jones wants 12 dozen fresh eggs put on board."

How in the world could I come up with 12 dozen fresh eggs? Then I remembembered the jewelry. I gave a handful of jewelry to my marine orderly and told him to take a jeep into the countryside and trade the jewels for fresh eggs. He came back with a big smile and plenty of eggs.

The Secret Service spelled out all the details of transporting the President. He would need to be lifted from his wheelchair and put in the Admiral's car. The armrest at the side of the back seat should be removed to avoid obstructing the President's entrance.

Well-Made Plans, Hazardous Passage

Most importantly, the ramp that went from the dock to the deck of the French destroyer could not be set at more than a five-degree incline. Otherwise, it would be too steep and dangerous for the President's descent by wheelchair to the ship's deck.

We studied the huge tides in the harbor and, as best we could, predicted where the deck of the destroyer would be at the time of the President's estimated time of arrival. Then we built a ramp long enough to maintain a five-degree incline, even if the President arrived an hour or so later than we planned.

The President landed in Dakar, and he was lifted into the Admiral's car without incident. The car proceeded to the harbor, and the road was lined with Senegalese soldiers, dressed in their red uniforms and standing at attention along the entire route.

When we arrived at the dock, the tide was cooperating. The President went aboard ship with no problem. After the rest of his party boarded, the destroyer pointed her bow out to the harbor where the USS Iowa was anchored. I knew it would be a long trip. Could it be possible that the Germans had learned of our plans? I couldn't relax until we came alongside the Iowa and the President was safely aboard.

> *In that one meeting in Dakar harbor, I came to like and respect the President. From that night on, I thought Franklin D. Roosevelt was a great President.*

On the way to the battleship, I heard the President ask Admiral Glassford who was responsible for his trip arrangements.

"My Flag Lieutenant."

The President responded, "I'd like to meet him."

When the Admiral called me over, the President put out his hand, and held mine in a very firm grip, not letting it go. He looked up from his chair and asked, "How are things going for you?"

"Fine, Mr. President."

The President then asked, "How's the mail? Are you getting your letters from home? How is communication with your family?"

I was really impressed. Of all the things President Roosevelt had to worry about — fighting and winning the war, getting enough supplies and personnel to Europe, and, most importantly, keeping peace among the Allies — he asked about my mail. He thought it was important that service people be able to keep in touch with home.

I was relieved when we arrived at the Iowa. The ship's crew had prepared a boatswain's chair for the President. It was a chair woven out of rope, attached to a davit, which they lowered onto the afterdeck of the destroyer. We tied the President into the chair, and the Iowa's crew hoisted him aboard.

Then we had an unexpected problem. How were we going to get all the top-ranking secretaries, generals and admirals on board? We had made plans for the President but not for his large entourage.

Walking the Plank

The Admiral ordered me to the bridge of the destroyer, so that I could help the French captain understand the Iowa captain, and vice versa. I headed to the bridge with a confident demeanor, as if I spoke fluent French. In reality, I knew almost no French and had to use sign language to communicate with the French captain. Fortunately, the President's entourage, whose lives were now in my hands, couldn't see me!

We finally tied the destroyer alongside the Iowa, so that its afterdeck house (the highest point on the destroyer with the exception of the bridge) was even with the lowest deck of the battleship. Then, with only about five feet between the ships, we connected both decks with a wide plank.

> *I think every man there knew that if President Roosevelt fell off the plank, he would never get out of that water alive.*

We arranged for two sailors on each ship to hold swabs (mops) alongside the plank, so that the dignitaries could hold the swabs while they negotiated the short trip to change ships. Fifty feet below the plank was white, churning water.

One by one, the men crossed over. One cabinet member even crawled across on his hands and knees. Thankfully, everyone crossed over safely.

Admiral Glassford related to me a conversation President Roosevelt and Prime Minister Churchill had before the beginning of the Casablanca conference.

"Where's de Gaulle?" asked President Roosevelt.

"He said he wasn't coming to Casablanca," replied Prime Minister Churchill.

"Who pays him?" asked Roosevelt.

"We do," responded Churchill.

"Where do you get the money?"

"From the United States."

Friendly Relationships

"All right, then," said Roosevelt, "Tell de Gaulle if he doesn't get himself down here, there will be no more money."

De Gaulle arrived the evening before the Casablanca Conference began.

During the time I was in Dakar, we travelled to a number of other African countries, some of which were well into the interior of the continent. Our job was to establish friendly relationships for the Allies with French- and British-controlled countries.

In 1944, President Roosevelt also charged us with convincing Liberia's new president, William Tubman, to declare war on Germany. The Allies needed to ferry A-2 bombers and other aircraft across the South Atlantic to Roberts Field in Liberia. However, Liberia was a neutral country, and according to the Geneva Convention, countries at war were not allowed to land planes in a neutral country.

I was reminded of my insignificance when I found myself at the very end of the table, seated next to the wife of the defeated candidate for president.

President Roosevelt named Admiral Glassford "Personal Representative to the President with the rank of Minister" to represent President Roosevelt at Tubman's inauguration. He also authorized him to promise President Tubman that the United States would build Liberia a ten-million-dollar airport if he declared war on Germany.

The evening before the inauguration, the president-elect held a huge dinner party at the Liberian "White House." We were told that Mrs. Tubman personally had baked an enormous cake for the occasion.

Everyone was seated with true protocol at a large table. The president-elect and first lady sat in the center, with the lesser lights, I among the least of them, sitting in descending order to the end of the table.

After dinner, the Admiral met privately with the President-elect and explained our proposal in detail. Tubman responded that we would have to wait for an answer until after his inauguration.

The following day we gathered with other dignitaries in a huge tent to celebrate the inauguration. It was extremely hot, and the President's speech went on and on, with no indication of how he felt about the Admiral's proposal.

After what seemed like hours, I suddenly heard President Tubman's voice saying " . . . and I don't like those Nazis. Wherever they go, they cause so much woe and misery!" I knew then that the Admiral had prevailed.

Within a few days, Liberia declared war on Germany. The United States kept its promise and began building a magnificent airport and harbor to facilitate transportation in this strategic country.

Some of my ambassadorial dealings were not so successful, as the following letter home will attest.

> My darling Ida,
>
> Four solid months in Dakar today — that's a long, long time.
>
> I just got in a little dutch with the boss . . . . He wanted to go horseback riding this afternoon and asked me to make arrangements for a French colonel to go with him. I telephoned the colonel and extended the A's invitation (all in French, as you no doubt have gathered). The colonel said that he understood, and I thought he did. But when the A went by for him at 10 minutes before five, the colonel was all set for a conference with the Admiral. I didn't know that my French was that bad.
>
> Well, such is life in French West Africa . . . If the heat doesn't get you, the language or the mentality of the ones the heat has already gotten, will do the job.
>
> > Love,
> > Allen

THE WORLD IN 1944

The tides of war had turned against the Nazi-Fascist Axis, and Allied forces were on the offensive around the globe. On June 4, American and British troops liberated Rome. On June 6, 250,000 Allied troops landed on the beaches of Normandy. It was D-Day, the largest combined land, sea and air operation in history, and the Allies' invasion of Western Europe had begun.

Despite these advances, the war was far from over. From Pas de Calais on the coast of France, the Germans continued to drop V-1 "Flying Bombs" on London at the rate of 100 a day. Each bomb carried nearly a ton of explosives. Allied casualties in Western Europe and in the Pacific reached record levels.

Still, the Allied advance continued. On August 24, General Charles de Gaulle liberated Paris, and by October the Allies had begun their invasion of Germany. On October 21, General Douglas MacArthur recaptured the Philippines, and American troops began fighting their way back across the Pacific.

A month later, Franklin Roosevelt was elected for his fourth term as President of the United States. "We have learned that we cannot live alone at peace, that our own well-being is dependent on the well-being of other nations far away," Roosevelt said in his inaugural speech. "We have learned that we must live as men, and not as ostriches, nor as dogs in the manger. We have learned to be citizens of the world, members of the human community."

CHAPTER SEVEN
The European Theater

On April 4, 1944, Admiral Glassford and I were ordered to return to Washington, D.C. We came back on a Pan American Clipper and stopped in Bermuda, where I bought 12 dozen cut Easter lilies for Ida, who met me at the Mayflower Hotel. The aroma of Easter lilies filled the hotel!

After reporting to President Roosevelt that our mission in Africa had been completed, Admiral Glassford was ordered to U.S. Naval Headquarters Europe in London. The Admiral was assigned to the staff of Admiral Harold R. Stark, Commander of the U.S. Naval Forces Europe. Our job was to help plan the Navy's role in the takeover of Germany, when the Germans surrendered.

The Bombing of London

We arrived during the bombing season, when the Germans were dropping V-1 and V-2 missiles on London, day and night.

The V-1 bombs were shaped like airplanes and fell around the clock. Clearly visible at low altitudes, they sounded like diesel engines at hard labor. They kept going until they ran out of fuel, and then they turned nose-down and headed for the ground, devastating everything within a few hundred feet from where they landed.

We learned not to worry as long as we could hear the engine

noise of the bombs. If you heard that noise stop, you knew you were likely to die.

The V-2s were another story. They carried much larger explosives than the V-1s, and they arrived silently and mostly at night. We compared them to a bolt of lightning: no warning, just an explosion.

Direct Hit

Most buildings had alarms that were activated when a V-1 was observed. Occupants were urged to move to the center of the building or to take shelter in the basement. We were warned about looking out windows: one blast could shatter glass for blocks away.

During this time, I had a flat (as we called our apartments in London) on the corner of Grosvenor Square and Carlos Street, catty-corner from the American Embassy. Six blocks away, on Duke Street, was Selfridge's Department Store.

There was a curfew in London, so by 11:00 o'clock in the evening, all the pubs closed and everyone was off the streets. One night, a few minutes after 11:00 p.m., a V-1 bomb hit a popular pub across from Selfridge's. I felt the blast in my flat, and the noise of the explosion was ear-shattering.

The bomb blew out the windows of the department store, sending mannequins flying into the street. Thankfully, no one was hurt, but the block was a frightening sight, with mannequin "bodies" strewn everywhere.

Adventure in the Azores

In February, 1945, Ida was expecting the arrival of our second child. I asked the Admiral if he could spare me for a trip home, and he said, "Write out the leave papers." He told me to do the job like any other job he had assigned me: as soon as it was finished, I was to return to London.

Getting back to the United States was a big problem. There were terrible storms in the North Atlantic, and planes could not land in Iceland, as they usually did.

After a few days of waiting, some airplanes were rerouted to the Azores, which are 800 miles off the coast of Portugal. I was able to get a seat, and we arrived at the islands in the middle of the night. Ida was due to begin her labor at any time, and I hoped that I could catch a plane home immediately.

There were some generals and other high-ranking officers who came in on a plane from Scotland. They were also heading for the United States, and they went immediately to the sergeant in charge of plane seats to point out how important they and their orders were.

Despite heavy pressure from the generals, the sergeant remained adamant: "There's nothing I can do for you. You know we don't have any extra space on our planes. Go up to the 'BOQ' [bachelor officers' quarters], and I'll call you as soon as something is available."

The high-ranking officers stomped out. Meanwhile, I had been sitting across from the sergeant's desk, half-asleep and watching their interaction. After a while, the sergeant and I were the only people left in the room.

"Aren't you going to the BOQ?" he asked. I told him that I was waiting until the commotion was over. "Anyway, I won't rate good quarters with all the generals there."

He asked me where I was headed. "Florida. I'm on leave, and I don't have any priorities."

"Why are you on leave?"

"My wife's expecting a baby."

"You see that plane out there? Go get on it!"

It was a hospital plane which had stopped for refueling. The plane was full of wounded soldiers from the Near East, and the small spaces between their bunks were occupied by nurses holding IV bags. There was no room for me to sit with them, so one of the officers told me to sit on my baggage in the back of the plane.

That's how I got to Newfoundland, and from there I flew to Washington and on to Tampa. Because of my uniform, everyone along was extremely courteous and helpful. As a result, I arrived home on February 16, 1945, just in time for Kay's birth.

As soon as Kay was born, I had to fly back to Washington for a return flight to London. The weather was still bad in the North Atlantic, and I was told I would have to wait in Washington until a flight was available.

To my surprise (because I had no priority), I was put on a plane that afternoon. The plane was full of Class I Priority boxes and crates of material heading for the war in Germany. I was the only passenger. That was a lonesome trip, sitting on a box by myself the whole night, and thinking about Ida and our little girls.

Shortly after I returned to London, Admiral Glassford was named Commander of U.S. Naval Forces in North African Waters (the Mediterranean). Our flagship was the USS Memphis, and we were ordered to Naples. We set up our shore headquarters in the city, after General Clark had driven the Italian army and navy north.

Prime Real Estate and Pasta

As flag lieutenant, I was responsible for finding appropriate headquarters for the admiral and his staff. I quickly learned where Italy's leading Fascists had lived (before they left in a hurry), and I requisitioned a beautiful home on the top of the Posilipo, a high hill with pretentious homes, overlooking the city of Naples and the bay. We also had a villa, "Quatro Venti," on the Isle of Capri, where the Admiral was able to spend a few weekends.

At the same time, I found the chief cook for the Italian admiral, who also had left Naples. I promptly installed this culinary expert in Admiral Glassford's kitchen, and he made great spaghetti with garlic sauce.

We'd never had it so good — especially after the poor food in Africa. The chef took great pleasure in creating masterpieces, and we took almost equal pleasure in eating them.

In Naples, one of my most unwarlike jobs was to host visiting congressmen, senators and other dignitaries from the United States. It was important for them politically to visit the war zone, and, in addition to seeing victory sites, they also wanted an audience with His Holiness, Pope Pius XII.

Visits to the Vatican

These visits to Vatican City, which had remained neutral throughout the war, were a highlight for me. The Pope was friendly and hospitable even to a lowly lieutenant commander — and a Protestant to boot!

The meetings always followed the same pattern. The attendant who opened the door did so with a flourish, ending up on his knees. The Pope rose from his chair and welcomed each visitor individually. Then he invited them to sit down for a discussion, and at the end of a short conversation, he gave out rosaries and religious medals and blessed them. This was how he ended the meeting.

The night before a visit to the Pope, a U.S. senator from a heavily-populated Catholic state asked me what would happen during the next day's visit.

Votes for Rosaries

I explained that His Holiness would probably give each member of the group a white rosary, a black rosary, and a few coins or medals with his likeness engraved on them. The Pope would then personally bless these items and any other religions objects in his visitor's possession.

"All other religious object on me?" the senator asked.

"Yes."

"Where can I get some of those beads?"

"How many do you want?"

"A hundred dollars worth!" he exclaimed and handed me the money in U.S. dollars.

Shortly, our orderly returned with a huge bag of rosaries. The next morning, the senator's pockets and waist were bulging. The Pope, true to form, blessed all the religious objects.

As we were leaving the Vatican, the senator said to me, "I'll never lose another election!"

And he never did.

THE WORLD IN
1945

In April, the Allies and the Red Army marched into Berlin; in August, the Japanese surrendered after Hiroshima and Nagasaki were leveled by atomic bombs. With the end of the war came joyous celebrations and somber assessments of the cost of battle. Over 70 million people had been killed in the war, including 13 million Chinese, 20 million Russians, 7 million Germans, and 300,000 Americans.

In the United States, Franklin Roosevelt had died in office after an unprecedented 13 years as President. Harry S. Truman was in the White House, and as Americans turned their thoughts to the future, millions of returning soldiers went to college on the GI Bill. Others returned to jobs with a standard 48-hour workweek and wages under one dollar an hour.

Meanwhile, using a technology learned during the war, American food processors pioneered a new drink — frozen orange juice. George Orwell published *Animal Farm*, and Rodgers and Hammersteins' *Carousel* was a Broadway hit. The song "June Is Busting Out All Over" captured the euphoria of the post-war era.

CHAPTER EIGHT
Moon Over Miami

I was in Naples when the war ended. I told the Admiral I would really like to go home, and he gave me permission to do so, after I found and trained my replacement. The Admiral then suggested that I take his plane for a two-week tour of Central Europe, but I said, "If it's all the same to you, Admiral, I just want to take a plane to the United States."

I flew from London to New York to Miami. Somewhere along the way, the Admiral sent me a telegram that said, "Thanks for everything!" It had been a great privilege and a tremendous education to serve with him during the war.

I returned to Atlanta in October 1945. I had three months accumulated leave, but after two weeks, I was ready to go back to work.

I spent several days looking for office space in downtown Atlanta, but it was an impossible task. There were no vacancies to be found. By this time, I was **Pens and Pencils** extremely restless and when I saw an ad for an advertising manager for Scripto Pens and Pencils, I applied. After hearing about my background in advertising, Scripto hired me on the spot, and I went to work the next Monday.

I only worked for Scripto for 15 months, but I loved it. In fact, it was a piece of cake — the company kept normal hours, so it wasn't necessary to work at night anymore. I contacted my friends in the drug and variety store chains, and our sales grew rapidly. I also redesigned Scripto's packaging and display material and named a new pen, the "Solidium," for its newly created metal.

A year later, in October, 1946, I met Ken Keyes at a luncheon in Atlanta. Mr. Keyes was a Miami Realtor who had developed a ministry of tithing. His talk, "In Partnership with God," served as a compelling challenge to Christians to tithe their income, and he was sharing his message with various churches across America.

A Life-Changing Encounter

Just prior to the luncheon, Mr. Keyes had learned from doctors in Warm Springs, Georgia, that his son, Ken, Jr. would be permanently paralyzed by polio. Ken was about my age, and Mr. Keyes was counting on him to take over his growing real estate business, so that he could focus on his ministry. When the doctors told him that Ken, Jr. probably would not regain enough use of his limbs to carry on a business career, Mr. Keyes knew that he would have to find someone else to direct his business or give up his ministry to churches altogether.

That night, Mr. Keyes called me at home at 11 p.m. "I've been talking to people in Atlanta about you all afternoon, and I'd like to meet you for breakfast at 7 a.m., before my train leaves," he said. I agreed, and to my surprise, over breakfast he asked me to come to Miami and take the job he had planned for his son.

I declined his offer. I explained that Ida and I had lived in Atlanta all our lives, that we were active in community affairs and had many lifelong friends in the city. Besides, I had been away for nearly five years in the service, and I really liked my work at Scripto.

In a few days, I received an eleven-page, handwritten letter from Mr. Keyes, offering me a great opportunity in real estate. I wrote back that I didn't know anything about real estate, and Mr. Keyes responded, "You know about advertising and selling. That's what real estate is!" As a result of his persistence, Ida and I agreed to visit Mr. and Mrs. Keyes in Miami in December, 1946.

During our visit, Ken threw a big party on the roof of the Everglades Hotel. The moon was full, the wind blew through the palm trees, and everyone was remarkably friendly. That night, Ida and I fell in love with Miami.

The next day we went to the Orange Bowl Game. The sun was shining, and I could smell the orange blossoms. I couldn't help but think of Atlanta with its sleet and freezing cold.

I was also impressed by some literature I read from Florida Power & Light. It said that only one percent of the earth's surface had a climate like Miami and that Miami was growing at a rate of nine percent a year. Any businessman would be encouraged by these superb conditions — a perfect climate and a growing population. Miami would need more houses and schools, stores and warehouses, and plenty of new businesses to support that growth.

As Ida and I drove down Biscayne Boulevard, she said, "This is one way to serve the Lord. If we move here to work with Mr. Keyes, this will give him the freedom to do what he does best — his talk on tithing."

We decided to accept Ken's offer and try it for a year. In February, 1947, we packed our furniture, and Ida, little Ida, Kay and I moved to Miami.

It was Ken Keyes who convinced me that tithing was something I could and should do. Ken's simple, yet effective, seminar talk focused on three points:

- All we have is given to us by God.
- God asks us to return 10 percent on his investment.
- His return is to be used in helping the poor and sharing our faith.

I always felt that, with a wife and two babies to support, I didn't have enough money to tithe. Just before we moved to

Eternal Investments

Miami, I was given a $2,000 bonus check from Scripto. Because of Ken's influence, I decided to give 10 percent of my bonus to the church. It was a one-time gift; I didn't intend to tithe my salary.

The week after I tithed my bonus check, I felt unusually happy. Good things began to happen. We sold our house in Atlanta by telephone, and in Miami, some friends found a house that we could move into right away. Everything seemed to fall into place so easily, and Ida and I were elated.

As a result of this experience, Ida and I decided to permanently adopt the practice of tithing.

Ken Keyes moved to Miami after World War I, at a time when the Florida land boom had gone bust. Many of the cities' office buildings stood empty. "I was broke and knew it," he told me. "Almost everyone else was broke but didn't know it yet."

Ken started a real estate listing business and made a meager living. In some cases, his commission for finding tenants was as high as 25 percent. After the Depression, when normal business conditions returned, he developed The Keyes Company with his main emphasis on real estate management.

Since that eventful time in February 1947, Ida and I continued to give the first 10 percent of our income to the Lord's work. Eventually, we increased our giving to 30 percent.

Real estate was a lot like marketing, and it didn't take me long to learn the business. I supervised the work of department heads and other vice presidents while Ken Keyes was out of town. During the first few years, Ken worked closely with me, but as business increased and his speaking engagements became more frequent, he devoted more and more time to his tithing ministry.

A Fast Start

During these early years, when Ken made a purchase for a client, I often ended up in charge of the project. Among other jobs, I supervised the Everglades Hotel, a laundry in Ocala, a tourist resort in Rainbow Springs, a radio station in Miami, WMBM, and a vending machine company.

I reported to Mr. Keyes on everything and was extremely busy. The first few years, I worked six days a week and sometimes on Sunday as well. None of this seemed like a hardship — I loved my work.

Early in our marriage, Ida and I decided that we would face all our problems as a team, sacrificing the present and always keeping our eyes to the future. During those years, I thought that my most important responsibility was to make a lot of money, so that

I could give my children a proper education and provide for future generations. I didn't want to be in the same position my father was in, when he had only $100 to give me for four years of college.

An Eye for the Future

Ida and I disciplined ourselves to save 15 percent of my earnings for insurance policies and small investments. Fortunately, we never felt a need to "keep up with the Joneses." Ida was an excellent manager of our home, and I often think that it was her frugality that enabled me to make real estate investments early in our family life.

With the money that Ida and I saved, I began investing in the area of Perrine and Homestead, Florida, for as little as $35 an acre. Certain that these investments would reap generous dividends, I bought land with down payments of 20 to 29 percent, with a three- to five-year payment plan. By 1990, the value of an acre in this area had reached $20,000, an increase of 5,700 percent in 43 years.

Because they were economical, codfish cakes were a weekly item on our dinner menu. I thought they were delicious.

We didn't know until our children were grown that they had a problem with codfish cakes. Their problem was that they hated them! Now that our adult children have admitted their dislikes, codfish cakes have become a family joke. When the children hosted our 50th anniversary party, they honored us with special hors d'ouvers: codfish cakes!

In an effort to understand Miami's real estate market, I devised a study called "A Township West of Miami." On a township map,

Investment Philosophy

for a number of years I recorded the sale price of an acre. For example, in 1947, one acre in South Dade County sold for $60. In 1948, the same acre went for $100. By the early 1950s, an acre sold for more than $500. Looking at the results of this study, anyone could see that real estate in South Dade County was an excellent, almost foolproof, investment.

Land speculation in Dade County was fairly easy because the county was laid out in grid sections of one square mile (640 acres) each. There are 36 sections to a township — 36 square miles. Main roads were always built on section lines and half section lines, so it was easy to locate where a road would be built.

My method for recommending land investments was simple. I monitored road construction to see where new expressways would be built. For example, Old Cutler Road became an interesting investment opportunity. Small tracts were offered for $500-600 per acre. It was almost "a sure thing" that the land's value would double in a year or two. People who invested at that time quickly doubled and even tripled their investments. Today, that same land is worth $400,000 or more an acre or more.

> *You could look at the use of adjoining properties to predict development trends. We recommended to our investors and developers that they buy property ahead of, and in the direction of, the area's growth.*

During the fifties, the primary direction of growth was north and south, because the Biscayne Bay was on the eastern border of Miami and the Everglades on the west. However, canals and drainage programs reclaimed thousands of acres of the Everglades. This enabled housing expansion to the west, and a great number of homes have been built in areas that were once swamplands.

Even in the early fifties, there were people who predicted that Miami's development eventually would form a great megatropolis, extending through Hollywood and Ft. Lauderdale all the way north to meet the development from Palm Beach. This has come to pass.

Miami has not grown as much toward the south and southwest because of the Everglades National Park.

Good Deed, Good Deal

One morning in the early fifties, Pete Catino, a salesman at The Keyes Company, came into my office looking heartbroken. "My wife told me this morning that she is going to leave me," he confided. "I haven't made a sale in nine months, and we don't even have enough money to pay the electric bill. I have good listings, but I can't find a buyer or close a deal."

I couldn't think of anything to cheer Pete up, so I asked him to show me his two best properties. The first was a group of stores on 27th Avenue that didn't have much appeal.

The second property, 230 acres in the Everglades, was even more discouraging. To get there, we drove out the Palmetto Expressway and then traveled on a berm alongside a canal as far as we could go, and when we climbed from the car, Pete pointed across the saw grass and a sea of water.

"See that little clump of trees about a mile over there?" he said. "That's the property."

What could I say to cheer Pete up? Who wants a property that's a mile away in a lake — and underwater?

We drove back to the office in silence. I started thinking, "If only Pete could make a sale, maybe it would change his luck. The sale price of the Everglades property is only $2,700 . . . guess I could afford that."

I told Pete to write up a contract on the 230 acres, and I would buy them. This simple little sale changed his luck. Pete began making deals again and saved his marriage.

To my surprise, Pete's Everglade property became one of the best real estate deals I ever made. I invited a friend to go in 50/50 with me, and as the years passed, the Snake Creek Canal was built. The canal drained off the water, and the land dried out.

Over the years, we traded some of the acreage, sold some for $1,000 an acre, and gave away quite a bit to church and charitable institutions. We had only a few acres left when the government planned to build the right of way for I-75 on our property.

The deal with Pete worked out well for everyone — that's my definition of a victory in real estate negotiations. Unfortunately, I never had a victory in agriculture.

In the Red with Tomatoes

During my first year in Miami, Ken Keyes pointed out that there would be many opportunities, aside from real estate, for investment. "We have some land down in South Dade County where we can plant tomatoes," he said. "We also have a farmer willing to do the work."

I put my entire life savings, $7,000, into the tomato business. Shortly afterwards, a flood in South Dade wiped out the entire crop. We planted a second crop, which was ruined by cold weather.

Our third crop was attacked by nematodes. We lost all three crops, and from that experience, I learned that God didn't want me to invest in farming!

During this period, Dewey Leader, the general manager of The Keyes Company, died of a heart attack. He was only 49 years old. Dewey was a great friend who taught me all he could about the real estate business, and I owed him a lot.

Shortly after Dewey's death, his brother offered his stock in The Keyes Company to Ken. When Ken declined, Dewey's brother offered it to me. Thanks to my tomato experience, I didn't

General Manager to President

have any money, but he agreed to let me pay for the stock over a period of years, with an interest rate of only 4.5 percent. With these shares, I now owned 49 percent of the company and Ken owned 51 percent. Ken then appointed me general manager.

In 1951, Ken called me and said the board of directors had decided to give me the job that went with what I was doing, so they named me president. By then The Keyes Company was the largest real estate business in South Florida, with an annual sales volume in excess of $21 million.

In 1951, I also became active in the Young President's Organization. The YPO was organized to bring experienced and successful businessmen together with younger people whose business experience had been delayed by their military service. At 38, I was one of the older "young presidents." I always enjoyed talking with and advising younger presidents at the YPO conventions and seminars, and I learned a lot from my peers. Members had to head a multimillion dollar business before they reached age 39, and they could continue their membership until the age of 49, when they were forced into retirement from YPO.

A year later our son was born. Of course I had no idea then that William Allen Morris, named for his maternal grandfather, William Akers, and for his paternal grandfather and his proud daddy, would himself one day serve as president of the Florida YPO while running the company that would bear my name.

In the early fifties, I learned from a friend in Atlanta that Southern Bell was looking for a building in the Miami area. I contacted them and found a suitable site, which they agreed to lease. The site was owned by a local banker, who agreed to construct a building to Southern Bell's specifications and lease it back to them for a 10-year period. The Keyes Company received a $17,000 commission for my work, which was a very large sum in those days.

At first, everyone was pleased with the deal. Within a few weeks, however, the banker sold the entire package to an investor. The new owner was happy to get a property with a 10-year lease from the phone company, which had a AAA credit rating and whose bonds were paying 5.5 percent.

Southern Bell, however, was not pleased to find themselves negotiating on the various aspects of construction with someone whom they had never met. "We don't like this one bit," the vice president told me. "Did you know that Joe Walker was going to sell the lease as soon as it was finalized?"

I assured him that I knew nothing about it and told him how sorry I was. "If you ever want to build again in South Florida, I'll personally find the site and erect the building, and handle the financing and leasing myself," I promised him. "I'll do it under the same terms as your lease with the banker, and I won't sell the property without your permission."

When I relayed this conversation to Ken, he told me he was not interested in real estate development; he only wanted to sell and manage other people's properties. "If you want to build, it's okay with me, as long as you pay the company the same commission they would earn if you were handling a sale or leasing for another investor."

Within a year, the Southern Bell real estate man called. He reminded me of my offer to be a builder-owner and asked me to build Southern Bell a complex in Ft. Lauderdale.

Shaky Beginnings

I entered this venture with no idea how to get the money for its completion. I put $500 down on the approved site and estimated that it would cost $70,000 to build. I explained to a friend, my partner in the project, that I thought we could borrow $60,000 from an insurance company. We would have to come up with $5,000 each.

As the building got bigger and bigger, I could see my estimate would be about $30,000 short. When I explained to my "would-be partner" that we would now need $15,000 each, he said, "Let me out. I didn't want to invest more than $5,000 in this project."

By Christmas 1954, the complex was far from finished. Our own household savings had dwindled to $2,000 when the architect called to say he needed some money for Christmas.

"How much?" I asked.

"Two thousand dollars will be about right."

"Great!" I responded confidently. "I'll send you a check." I took the last $2,000 from our savings to pay him, leaving our household with little cash for the holidays.

I was still wondering where I would get the other $30,000. I tried all the sources I knew, but there just wasn't any money available. Then I thought of Comer Kimball, chairman of the First National Bank (later

"A Tide in the Affairs of Men"

known as the Southeast Bank), with whom I had worked on Red Cross, Community Chest and University of Miami projects. I invited Comer to lunch at the Miami Club. I was too nervous to eat very much, so I was relieved when he finished eating and lit his cigar.

I told Comer that when I was at Boys' High in Atlanta, I had an English professor who made us memorize certain passages of Shakespeare. I began to quote, "There is a tide in the affairs of men/Which taken at the flood leads on to fortune . . "

To my surprise, Comer continued the quote, ". . . Omitted, all the voyage of their life/Is bound in shallows and in miseries." He told me that he too had gone to Boys' High and studied with the same English teacher.

"What is the 'tide' in your life?" he asked.

I told him the whole story, how the building grew in size

This one loan was pivotal for my whole career, and it came to me through poetry.

and I lost my partner and needed $30,000. Comer said he would look into it and would call me later in the afternoon.

Somehow I knew, when he finished the quotation from Brutus' speech in Act IV of *Julius Caesar*, that I had the money. Sure enough, that afternoon the vice president of the bank called to say he had $30,000 for me.

Despite its shaky beginning, the Southern Bell project turned out well. The building was con-

New Opportunities

structed for $9 a square foot and is still there today, totally renovated and re-leased to new tenants. (Back then, I thought that in 20 years the building would probably be worth about half its construction cost. I had no idea how much inflation and population would affect its value. Today, it would cost $80-90 a square foot to put up a similar building.)

The Southern Bell project led to opportunities to bid on other projects. Ultimately, we were the successful bidders on many other buildings, and our tenants included Florida Power and Light, Tropical Gas, Florida Gas, Travelers Insurance, Bank of America, General Motors, The Federal Reserve Bank, Unisys, and IBM. Because I could earn enough to take care of my family by running The Keyes Company, I didn't need to make an immediate profit from the buildings. My philosophy was to charge only enough rent to carry the mortgage, and as a result, I was usually the lowest bidder.

Every time I built a new building, I began a new corporation. I did this for two reasons. First, in the 1950s, the tax laws exempted corporations from paying taxes on their first $5,000 in profits. Secondly, I usually had to borrow all the money for a building project. With separate corporations, if one building failed, I would lose only that building — not four or five others. At one point I had 30 different corporations. I paid The Keyes Company the same commission due them as if I had been representing a client, and this arrangement proved to be advantageous for both of us.

The Keyes Company prospered as it grew to new millions in sales and leases. I remained there for 11 years, seven of them as president. Some of our projects were more successful than others, but all were educational, and they set the stage for the next important change in my life.

THE WORLD IN
1958

In Europe, General Charles de Gaulle was elected the first president of France's Fifth Republic. Nikita Khrushchev became the premier of the Union of Soviet Socialist Republics, and Fidel Castro launched a guerrilla war against the government of Cuba.

Despite the shadow of the Cold War, in the United States, it was a time of peace and prosperity. A World War II hero, General Dwight D. Eisenhower, was serving his second term in the White House. The United States launched its first satellite and established the National Aeronautics and Space Administration (NASA) to conduct the scientific exploration of outer space.

In the arts, *West Side Story* played on Broadway, and Boris Pasternak published *Dr. Zhivago*. Music lovers purchased their first "stereophonic" records, and the counter-culture "Beatnik" movement, which began in California, swept through the United States and Europe.

CHAPTER NINE
The Allen Morris Company

By 1958, The Keyes Company's annual sales volume had reached $75,000,000. The business was in good financial shape, and the vice presidents were all great people: experienced, capable and a joy with whom to work.

At the time, my biggest project was financing, building and leasing the Northside Shopping Center. It was an enormous task, and before long, I knew that I would have to choose between developing Northside or remaining as president of The Keyes Company. I chose the former, and in 1958, I started my own real estate business, The Allen Morris Company.

It was the great twentieth century industrialist, Arthur Vining Davis, founder of the Aluminum Company of America (ALCOA), who introduced me to the concept of regional shopping centers. Mr. Davis was one of the richest men in the world, and although he was about 80 years old when he moved to Miami, he had a sharp mind and an uncanny ability to predict the direction of the city's growth.

Opportunity Knocks

I first met Mr. Davis in the early fifties at an opening of his Arvida dairies in North Dade County. ("Arvida" was an acronym for Arthur Vining Davis.) I met him again, when I was calling on prospective donors for the United Fund and the American Red Cross.

Two years later, I was at a party when someone told me that Mr. Davis was going to buy the Metropolitan Bank. I had a listing on a property next to the bank, so early the next morning, I sent Mr. Davis a letter offering him the property. I asked him to call me if he was interested.

At 10 a.m., my secretary, Mrs. Jordan, interrupted a staff meeting to tell me I had a call from Mr. Davis. "I have your letter," he said. "Can you come over and tell me about the property?"

"Yes sir!" I exclaimed. "I'll be there in two minutes."

I adjourned the meeting, rushed out the back door,

> *The quality of a man's life is in direct proportion to his commitment to excellence.*

sprinted three blocks to the Dupont Building, rode the elevator to the 16th floor and walked into Mr. Davis' reception room. There stood Mr. Davis with his pocket watch in hand.

He laughed and said, "I knew you couldn't be here in two minutes!"

Arthur Vining Davis founded the Aluminum Company of America shortly after he graduated from Amherst College at the age of 18. He formed the company in Pittsburgh with a young chemist, Charles Martin Hall, who had developed a process to separate aluminum ore from bauxite. He had successfully used the aluminum to make cooking pots and frying pans.

Alfred E. Hunt was in charge of the company, and Mr. Davis and Mr. Hall were in control of production. They each worked 12-hour shifts, seven days a week, to keep the fur-

Pots, Pans and Pineapples

nace going. They developed some experimental cooking utensils that Mr. Davis' mother said were the best she had ever used.

When they realized that they needed capital to expand this business, Mr. Davis told me he had approached the Mellon Bank with a business plan. Mr. Davis came back the next morning, and Mr. Mellon told him that he had not asked for enough money. He said, "My brother and I believe it will take twice as much as you have asked for, and we are prepared to lend it to you." Mr. Davis and his partner continued to operate the company in a very frugal way.

I learned firsthand of Mr. Davis' financial acumen when, in the early fifties, an associate of The Keyes Company sold him a large tract of land west of Boca Raton. Mr. Davis bought the land for $40 an acre and sold it for $1,000 per acre. Land in this area is now worth hundreds of thousands of dollars per acre!

Later, he paid $60 an acre for a pineapple plantation in North Dade County. The land is now the location for the largest interchange of expressways in South Florida. A recent sale in the area was at $14 a square foot. As Ken Keyes used to say, "The secret is to buy land by the acre and sell it by the square foot."

Mr. Davis knew from experience what happens when cities grow and their expanding population needs more and more land. I talked to him one day after he had just paid $1,500 an acre for some land west of the Miami Airport.

"Isn't that a lot of money?" I asked.

"Imagine if you owned property this close to the courthouse in Pittsburgh," Mr. Davis replied. "What would it be worth today?"

Today, the land west of the airport is selling from $10 to $15 per square foot — $400,000 to $600,000 an acre.

Mr. Davis made money, but he also gave it away. He was a great contributor to Third World countries. He didn't simply send money; he sent care packages which included tools and seeds for farming. He was also a substantial contributor to the restoration of the Agora, an ancient marketplace located at the foot of the Acropolis in Athens, Greece.

Although Mr. Davis did not buy the property I offered him, we became friends almost immediately. He had a great sense of humor and loved to laugh. Our business relationship was simple — Mr. Davis told me what land he wanted, and I got it for him!

When his purchase of the Metropolitan Bank was finalized, Mr. Davis asked me to be on his board.

"I really appreciate your offer, Mr. Davis, but I'm already on the board of a bank," I replied. Regulations prohibited an individual from serving on bank boards under different ownership.

"You can resign, can't you?"

"Yes sir," I replied. I promptly resigned from the bank to join his board.

I will never forget the first board meeting of the Metropolitan Bank. It started at 4 p.m. and ended at 5:30. Mr. Davis thanked the acting chairman for a fine meeting but added that his idea of a board meeting was one that lasted less than an hour.

From then on, the preliminary work and recommendations were completed by committees, whose chairmen gave their reports at the meeting. As a result, the directors completed their meetings in record time.

A Minute Saved

One day in the late 1950s, Mr. Davis asked me to arrange a $10 million loan so that he could buy a large tract of land. I had some friends at Prudential Insurance Company in New Jersey, and I thought they might be interested. A few days later, Mr. Davis and I boarded one of his planes to New York. He owned a DC 3, a small plane and two helicopters.

When we arrived, Mr. Davis went to the apartment he maintained on Park Avenue, and I went to the Waldorf-Astoria Hotel. The next morning, to my surprise, Mr. Davis was waiting for me in the lobby to wish me a successful meeting with Prudential. It was successful — Prudential made a verbal commitment to lend the $10 million.

Arthur Vining Davis was 85. Imagine making million dollar deals and buying large tracts of land at that age!

Meanwhile, one of Mr. Davis' friends from First Boston Corporation learned of his need for $10 million. He suggested that Mr. Davis sell some of his ALCOA stock instead of borrowing money. Mr. Davis owned more than 1,000,000 ALCOA shares. His cost was only one cent per share. In the late 1950s, this stock was selling for $135 per share. Mr. Davis took his friend's advice and sold some of his ALCOA stock.

Before long, Mr. Davis began talking to me about shopping centers. "Right now, regional shopping centers are a fad," he said, "but they are here to stay. Miami has only one regional shopping center. I'd like to build three more, and I'd like you to develop them for me."

I was startled. "I appreciate your confidence, Mr. Davis, but I don't know a thing about regional shopping centers."

"You can learn, can't you?"

"Yes, sir." I said. And I did.

Negotiating the leases was extremely stressful work. We had to meet the requirements of the mortgage company as well as our own budget, and we had to have the right mix of stores to appeal to the consumer.

> *I couldn't start construction until I had financing, and I couldn't get financing until I had a certain number of AAA-credit tenants signed up.*

A large national retailer insisted on having one of the best locations in the mall. For that privilege, I felt they should pay five percent of their sales in rent. However, the company's leasing representative claimed that they had never paid such a high percentage at any location.

I thought I remembered a conversation with a friend at a commercial property clinic in Chicago, where I was told that the tenant had a lease at five percent in a shopping center in Minneapolis. I called my friend, and he confirmed this information.

At my next meeting with the company's leasing representative, I told him I was not leasing the space to him for less than five percent. He continued to insist that the company never paid that much. "What about Minneapolis?" I asked. He was shocked that I knew about this arrangement, and we settled on a five percent lease.

Prudential Insurance Company insisted that I get minimum rent guarantees from my AAA credit tenants. However, in my negotiations with Sears, the store was only willing to pay a minimum rent if they had a rent cap of $300,000 a year. Without a minimum rent, they were willing to pay 2.25 percent of their sales.

I was confident that Sears would do a lot of business, and that on a straight percentage, their rent could go as high as $500,000 a year. Prudential insisted on having a minimum, but after many weeks and many flights between Chicago and Newark, I was able to negotiate a compromise. It was one of the best deals I ever negotiated: Sears agreed to pay a straight percentage of 2.25 percent, with no minimum. They also agreed to pay a minimum of

$156,000 a year with a maximum of $300,000 a year if I ever was in default on the Prudential mortgage. This agreement satisfied all parties and the lease was signed. Under this arrangement, Sears paid as much as $600,000 rent in a single year.

At one point during the construction of Northside Shopping Center, I had borrowed all the money I could from the two biggest banks in Miami, and I still needed $400,000 to complete the building.

Gentleman's Agreement

I called Mills Lane, who was chairman of the Citizens & Southern Bank in Atlanta and told him I needed $400,000 for six months. The most I had ever borrowed from C&S was $1,500, and that was 19 years earlier when I opened my advertising agency.

Mills suggested that I come see him early the next morning. "I'll be in my office at 6:30 a.m," he said.

I flew to Atlanta, and at 6:30 a.m., the security guard let me in the bank. I told Mills why I needed the money and how I was going to pay it back. He said, "Okay, you've got it." We shook hands, and as I walked out the door, he added, "Oh, I'm going to have to charge you six percent interest." If you told anyone today that that's how we did business back then, I doubt they would believe you!

Walter Etling and I went to New York to wrap up the Woolworth lease. We met the chairman and president, and then went into a conference with the real estate vice president on the top floor of the Woolworth Building.

During our lease negotiations, I felt a sharp chest pain. I wanted to conclude our meeting as soon as possible. We were at the end of two years of tough negotia-

Home Remedies for a Heart Attack

tions, and finally we came down to seven points on which we couldn't agree. I said, "You take four and give me the other three." The leasing representative agreed, and we made the lease. By this time I had learned that compromise, which is so important in business and in life, is simply give-and-take. Of course, one never compromises on points of moral-ity or principles, but in most situations, there is a middle ground. In this case, it was more important to close the deal than to win on every point.

We then rushed out to keep our lunch appointment with a vice president of Newberry's. After lunch, we visited Newberry's store in a new shopping center in New Jersey.

The pain was worse, so we stopped in a drugstore, where I took some aspirin and drank a Coca-Cola. A few hours later, I caught a plane to Chicago to meet with Lerner's real estate vice president.

When I arrived in Chicago, I still had chest pains. I didn't want to go to the hospital there, so I took a couple of aspirin and drew a tub of hot water, soaking in the bath until the water cooled off. I repeated this procedure several times for the next 24 hours.

When I returned to Miami, my doctor gave me an EKG. I had taken a physical one month earlier, and he said, "You've had a heart attack since you left here."

I've always believed that the combination of hot water baths and aspirin is what saved me from a more critical problem. According to my doctor, the aspirin thinned my blood and lying in a tub of hot water dilated my blood vessels, taking a load off my heart. It was clearly a situation where the Lord looked after me.

> *I went to the hospital and slept for five days. The first thing I saw when I woke up was a photograph of Ida and the children. It was a timely reminder of what is important in life.*

The doctor told me to go to Victoria Hospital. I agreed, "I'll go back to the office and get some things done, and check in around six or seven this evening."

"Who's going to be your doctor?" he asked me.

"You are, of course."

"Not I," he said, "unless you go to the hospital right now."

After I left the hospital, I quickly plunged back into lease negotiations. We needed one more major variety store with AAA credit, and Woolworth's agreed to have a Newberry's department store. Just as Newberry's president was about to sign our lease, Mr. Newberry walked in to the president's office and said, "I'm concerned about the economy. Don't sign any more leases."

With Newberry's gone, Woolworth's suggested that we approach Grant's department store. I didn't think Grant's was strong enough (within a year, they were bankrupt), so I turned to Kresge's variety store. Their vice president of real estate was extremely interested. I asked him whether he could sign a lease within 24 hours if I came to Detroit the next day. The vice president agreed. I flew to Detroit, and by 5:00 o'clock that evening, he had signed the lease, subject to Woolworth's approval.

I flew back to Woolworth's and told them we had a problem but also a solution. "I have a lease signed by Kresge's, which is subject to your approval. But if we can't have this lease, we aren't going to have a shopping center." Woolworth's accepted the lease, subject to Kresge's agreeing to have no more than 50 seats in their restaurant, because Woolworth's wanted the largest restaurant in their own store. Kresge's said okay. We qualified for the mortgage and started construction.

Despite my heart attack, Northside Shopping Center went ahead as planned, with approximately 70 stores ready for business in March, 1960. The Sears store there was the second largest east of the Mississippi.

While we were building Northside, the architects were planning Dadeland shopping center, and we were negotiating leases with the top tenants. As soon as Northside opened, I began having second thoughts about the stress connected with developing another regional shopping center.

Grand Openings

About this time, Mr. Davis decided to sell his Arvida holdings. One of these was Dadeland. I sold my interest in Dadeland to the new officers of Arvida. Dadeland became one of the largest and most successful malls in the United States today.

Now that I was concentrating on developing office buildings instead of shopping malls, in 1960, in anticipation of inflation, I began writing in escalation clauses in our leases. For some reason, however, in 1963, I rented a building for 15 years, without any escalation clause.

Within the next ten years, inflation caused the cost of electricity, cleaning services, taxes and miscellaneous management expenses to skyrocket. For the last five years of the lease, the services for the building alone cost more than the total rent, and we received absolutely no profit for all our work.

Despite occasional setbacks, the Allen Morris Company continued to prosper. One important reason for our success was my outstanding secretary, Mrs. Katie Jordan. Mrs. Jordan began working for me shortly after I arrived in Miami and remained with me for almost 30 years.

Behind Every Good Man . . .

She doubled my efficiency, and because people liked her, they liked doing business with me.

Mrs. Jordan put up with my perfectionism — her nickname for me was "Simon Legree" — and she was always anxious to get the day's work done. More than once, after we had negotiated a lease, she brought her notebook into my office and said, "Let's write up the leasehold agreement right now." She stayed after hours to complete the agreement and deliver it to the post office. The next morning, the customer found it on his desk. The customer then looked good to his boss and his associates, but it was Mrs. Jordan who was the real hero!

By the mid-sixties, the Allen Morris Company was in a strong position. In 1966, we sold Northside Shopping Center for 12 million. In the same year, I was elected president of the National Institute of Real Estate Brokers, a 17,000 member organization. I was also head of 19 other real estate corporations in Florida, as well as chairman of the board of the Northside Bank in Miami — so I did not have a lot of spare time.

In 1967, we received a $2.8 million loan to build a new highrise office building at 1000 Brickell Avenue. Ground was broken on November 22, 1967, and our key tenant was Travelers Insurance Company.

Despite these many successes, there was still something missing in my life. In the spring of 1967, at Arrowhead Springs, California, I found out what that something was.

Remembering Thirty Years of Service

by Mrs. Katharine Jordan

I started working for Mr. Morris as his secretary in June of 1948, and I was almost 70 when I retired 30 years later. He is one of the most brilliant men I've ever known.

When I made mistakes, he never talked about them in front of anyone. He would take the blame for anything that went wrong, and that's very unusual. He had a way of making you feel loyal by always building you up around other people.

We both worked long hours. I arrived at the office early, around 7 a.m., and Mr. Morris was usually already there. I've even had him call me at 3:00 a.m., when he was on the West Coast, and ask me to do something! He seldom made it home for meals, and he worked Saturdays and Sundays. All of this was awfully hard on the family, but Ida Morris never complained. She was terrific!

Mrs. Morris had a tremendous influence on him and the children. It was she who was there for Ida and Kay and Allen while Mr. Morris was busy making money.

Mr. Morris was the most economical person you've ever heard of. I sent Mrs. Morris her houseold spending money once a month, and it wasn't very much. Once, I asked her if she wanted to borrow some money from me, and she thought that was so funny. When the Morrises' son, Allen, was at Georgia Tech, Mr. Morris gave him only $100 a month. I thought that wasn't enough, and he told me, "If you want to spoil a boy, have one of your own!"

I'm now 85 years old, and last Christmas I decided to fly down to Miami and go to my lifelong church. Because I have no family, I called one of the women in the Allen Morris Company and asked her if she would meet me at the airport. When I got there, Allen Morris was there to greet me. He took me to see Kay's family and then Allen's, and I ended up getting to church 15 minutes late. I thought it was the sweetest thing, that he would take so much time on Christmas Day!

THE WORLD IN
1967

Long-standing tensions erupted in the Middle East. Israel fought a brief, "Six-day War" with its Arab neighbors and occupied the West Bank of Jordan and the Golan Heights. The Soviet Union and the United States remained locked in a nuclear stalemate, and the Cold War found a flash point in the rice paddies of Vietnam.

In the United States, Lyndon Johnson was President. The civil rights movement, led by Martin Luther King, Jr. was at its crest, and an anti-war movement swept the country. For the first time in American history, the use of illegal drugs became widespread among young people.

In the same year, *You're a Good Man, Charlie Brown* was a hit musical, and Dustin Hoffman starred in *The Graduate*. The Beatles and The Rolling Stones dominated popular music. Mickey Mantle hit his 500th home run, and Dr. Christian Barnard performed the first human heart transplant.

CHAPTER TEN
A Spiritual Journey

Just before Easter 1967, I received an invitation from Campus Crusade for Christ to attend an executive seminar in Arrowhead Springs, California. At the time, I was president of the National Institute of Real Estate Brokers and already scheduled to speak in Las Vegas and Anaheim, California. The Campus Crusade seminar was only a few miles from Anaheim and scheduled for the days between my speaking engagements.

"What a coincidence," I thought. "I'd rather go to a Campus Crusade seminar than fly back to Miami for just a few days."

Looking back, I can see it was all arranged by God!

After dinner on my first night at Arrowhead Springs, Dr. Bill Bright delivered an inspiring message about "the cleansed life." Bill was the founder and president of Campus Crusade, and Ida and I had met him and his wife, Vonette, seven years earlier (1960) at a lay retreat. I have admired Bill and his ministry ever since.

The next morning, Henrietta Mears, the famous Bible teacher from Hollywood Presbyterian **Reluctant Trainee** Church, delivered a stirring devotional. After breakfast, we were asked to spend a half hour in silence, contemplating Miss Mears' message.

This was a completely new experience for me. I had lived my whole life "on the run." "How can I spend an entire half hour doing nothing?" I asked myself. There was no telephone or television — just quiet. The time passed slowly, and I found it hard to concentrate.

After our quiet time, we divided into groups of eight. A Campus Crusade instructor passed out little booklets entitled, *The Four Spiritual Laws.* "You need to learn these well before we go witnessing this afternoon," he said.

His words were a bombshell. Like the line from *Casey at the Bat,* "a pallor wreathed the features" of everyone in the room.

Witnessing? Me?

My first thought was to call my secretary, Mrs. Jordan. Surely she could send me a telegram, telling me to return to Miami immediately! Unfortunately, there was no graceful way to exit the room. Feeling trapped, I picked a lawyer to be my partner, hoping that he could handle the hard part.

My partner and I approached our first house. We agreed that he would stand by and pray while I witnessed. Much to my amazement, the first man with whom we spoke allowed us to share the plan of salvation.

After we practiced witnessing, we were served a light salad for lunch. I noticed how little everyone ate — apparently I wasn't the only one who was scared almost to death. I tried to comfort myself with the thought that I was 3,000 miles from home, and no one would know me.

At the next house, it was my turn to pray. I followed a practice that I still use today. Breathing out, I asked God to forgive my sins. Then breathing in, I asked God to fill me with the Holy Spirit. This practice, which Bill Bright calls "spiritual breathing," is based on I John 1:6 *Living Bible,* ". . . if we confess our sins to Him, he can be depended on to forgive us and to cleanse us from every wrong." Also Ephesians 5:18 — "Be filled instead with the Holy Spirit and controlled by him." As a result, I felt much more confident in my witnessing. We continued to knock on doors, explaining to people how they could invite Christ into their lives.

That afternoon of witnessing was more life changing than any event since my conversion as a child. I suddenly felt that I had a new, vivid and personal relationship with Christ. To this day, I believe that sharing Christ with others is the best way to feel close to Him. In this way, we do what God wants us to do: we pass on the story, His story.

A Change of Heart

With the change in my relationship to Christ, I felt a new appreciation for people. In all honesty, my attitude towards others had been shaped largely by mass advertising. I saw people as consumers, a market for the product I was selling. Now I began seeing people more personally, as human beings with feelings and needs and souls to be saved. I realized that many people really want to invite Christ into their lives — but just don't know how.

As I matured in Christ, I began praying for my friends and others whom I felt did not know the Lord. I felt responsible for telling them how to accept Christ, and I shared with them two booklets that Bill Bright had written: *The Four Spiritual Laws* and *Jesus and the Intellectual*. Over the years, I developed a love for people, and I tried to share Christ with them, even if they were perfect strangers.

Stand-In for the Lord

After my experience at Arrowhead Springs, I decided that the only reason I was elected president of the National Institute of Real Estate Brokers was so that I could deliver a message on behalf of the Lord. A week later, when the main speaker was held up in a snowstorm, I was asked to give the keynote address at the Oklahoma State Convention.

I combined my standard real estate talk with elements about the economy, some sales and marketing techniques, and my thoughts on our responsibility to help others in our respective communities. Then, I spoke about inflation, which was just becoming a problem. "Haircuts used to cost a quarter; now they cost a dollar. In five years, you'll pay $5 for a haircut." No one believed me!

I also pointed out the great need for Christian principles and ethics in our country — especially in our everyday business life. I ended my talk with the quote from Joshua 24:15, "As for me and my house, we will serve the Lord." When I spoke about Christ, the response was unbelievable. In fact, I had never seen anything like it. Many of those businessmen and women had not been exposed to the Gospel. Everything had always been strictly business; now they wanted to talk more about my faith than about real estate.

Whenever I mentioned tithing, after my talk, a crowd usually gathered to ask me questions. They wanted to know how much they should give to God and how to determine to whom or what organizations their money should be given. It was a real joy to talk with these people.

I might never have begun my journey were it not for Ida's prayers and, seven years earlier, Vonette Bright's bringing her to the Lord. Ida explains:

God's Plan and Answered Prayers

The first time I met Vonette Bright, she asked me if I was sure of my salvation. I said, "I didn't know that I could be sure!"

"You can be absolutely certain," she responded. "The first step is to ask God to forgive your sins."

She lost me right there. I knew I was not a sinner — I hadn't killed anyone or stolen anything.

Vonette must have known what I was thinking. "Do you know what sin is?" she asked. It seemed like a silly question to me, but she continued. "Sin is anything we do or think that is not the will of God. It's losing our temper, gossiping, having a big ego. But one of the worst sins is worry."

"Oh gracious, this lady must know me!" I thought. "I've done all those things."

Vonette went on to explain that becoming a Christian was as simple as inviting Jesus into my heart. I didn't really believe her, but she had planted a seed.

Allen and I found out that the Brights would be in Miami after the conference, to set up a Campus

Crusade ministry at the University of Miami. We invited them to stay in our home. Our entire family was drawn to them, because we had never heard anyone talk about Jesus the way they did.

When I was driving Bill and Vonette to the airport for their return to California, Bill shared with me the plan of salvation. This time I understood. I could hardly wait to get home! As soon as I arrived, I knelt at my bed and asked Jesus to forgive my sins. "Please come into my heart and make me the kind of person You want me to be."

I honestly didn't know what I had done, if anything. It wasn't long, however, before God gave me the peace that passeth understanding. A deep joy began to run through my life — and still does. I realized I didn't have to keep pushing and trying to do everything. God was in control of my life, and he would allow only what was best for me.

Then I began to wonder, "Why hasn't anyone ever told me this before? Here I am 42 years old, and I'm just understanding God's plan of salvation."

I thought about all the other people in the world like me. God put them on my heart so heavily that I knew I needed to share the plan of salvation — and I've been sharing it ever since. If I'm not going out to meet someone, I pray that God will send people into my life who need to hear the Gospel — and He does.

Soon after Bill and Vonette's visit, Campus Crusade sent Eddie Waxer to the University of Miami. Because of his influence, all our children prayed the prayer for salvation. Big Allen, at that time, was still so oriented toward work and money that he didn't take much time for spiritual things.

One day, I said, "Lord, I've been praying for Allen for seven years. Please take him and help him do something big for you, because he won't be happy with anything less."

Two weeks later, Allen came home and announced

he had been elected president of the National Institute of Real Estate Brokers. "I'll be flying all over the country speaking, and I want you to go with me," he said. "But I don't want you to go around witnessing to everyone! Understand?"

I didn't say anything, because I knew I wasn't going to keep quiet. I kept praying for Allen and shortly afterwards, he got his invitation to Arrowhead Springs. When he came back, he had a new zeal to tell people about the Lord.

A week later, he was asked to speak at a real estate convention in Tulsa. He spoke about being a Christian businessman and ended with "As for me and my house, we will serve the Lord." Afterwards, someone asked me, "How long has your husband been religious like this?" I said, "Since last week!"

Allen traveled all over the country, giving his inspiring message. Needless to say, I was one joyous wife.

Before long, I was witnessing to close friends and family members. One night, over dinner in New York, I introduced Don Woodward to *The Four Spiritual Laws.*

Sewing Seeds, Reaping a Harvest

Don was an investment counselor who was respected in financial circles around the world.

When we said good night, I had no idea how Don felt about our conversation. Two years later, Bill Bright mentioned to me that he had visited with Don. Bill had asked him his favorite question, "Are you sure you'll go to heaven when you die?"

Don answered, "Yes, I am."

Bill asked, "How long have you been sure?"

Don replied, "I invited Christ into my life two years ago when I had dinner with Allen Morris in New York!"

Within a few years, Don died of a heart attack in San Diego. I'm so grateful he had the assurance that he would spend eternity in heaven with Jesus Christ.

Closer to home and even dearer to my heart, in 1967, I was

able to witness to my brother-in-law, Johnny Houser. Johnny was editor of Hollywood's *Variety Daily*, which was considered *the* newspaper in the entertainment world.

I met with Johnny and my sister, Kit, at my mother's home in Pasadena. I was eager to share with them the things I had learned at Arrowhead Springs, and I walked them through *The Four Spiritual Laws*. When I asked them if they wanted to invite Christ into their lives, they both responded, "Yes." I think it was the first time my sister realized the true meaning of having a personal relationship with Christ.

Soon afterwards, Kit and Johnny moved to Calhoun, Georgia, where Johnny became associated with the local newspaper. He wrote several books and even dedicated one to me, "because he introduced me to Jesus Christ."

After my mother died, Kit and Johnny moved back to California. Sometime later, Johnny was diagnosed with cancer of the esophagus. My sister called and said, "Johnny wants you to come see him, so that he can to talk you before he dies."

I caught the next plane to Los Angeles and went to his hospital room. "Thank you for coming," Johnny said. "I wanted to thank you for telling me about God's plan of salvation, and I want you to know that I am not afraid to die, because I know I will be with Jesus."

That experience far overshadowed any real estate deal I had ever made. In fact, there is no comparison. When the end came, my brother-in-law died a peaceful death. Now he's in heaven, and I know I will see him there some wonderful day.

When we first started sharing the plan of salvation with people, Ida and I were both hesitant. I was afraid of rejection and embarrassment, but I quickly found out the truth — people desperately want to hear about Christ.

To the Ends of the Earth

How should we witness? Jesus says in the Great Commission, "To the ends of the earth about my death and resurrection" (Acts 1:8 *LB*). Peter and John tell us that the desire to witness becomes irrepressible. "For we cannot stop telling about the wonderful things we saw Jesus do and heard him say" (Acts 4:20 *LB*). Unlike the early Christians, we don't endanger our lives every time we tell someone about Christ.

I'm convinced that the best place to share the Gospel is on an airplane. A lot of people are scared to death when they fly and are willing to talk to anyone!

There are other ways to witness. One lady from our church drives a van loaded with soup and peanut butter and jelly sandwiches to blighted areas of Miami each day. Homeless people wait for her every afternoon, and if she doesn't appear, they go without food. This "missionary" always takes other Christians along, so they can share the joy of meeting people's needs in Christ's name. She does all this after finishing her regular job at the U.S. Post Office.

> *Ida and I ask for opposite aisle seats, so we can both sit next to someone with whom we can share the plan of salvation. We always bring along* **The Four Spiritual Laws** *booklets, which we use as an introduction.*

Witnessing is simply allowing the Lord to use us to convey His words. In this effort, it is natural for us to feel inadequate or unworthy — because we are. However, Jesus promised, "The Holy Ghost will come upon you." When we are filled with the Spirit, we have the power of God within us.

God has made provision for those of us who may not yet be ready to share the plan of salvation. Paul teaches that, if you can't go yourself, you should send someone else. There are literally thousands of people all over the world who have a compulsion to share the plan of salvation with others. These people would never have the means to "tell the Good News" if there weren't other people to send them.

The fact is that most of us are "sending type" Christians. Being a "sender" is a great mission that brings great joy. Just a few dollars to foreign missions may make it possible for someone in a faraway place to learn of the love of Jesus Christ.

Sometimes I wake up at night and think, "Even now while I'm here in a nice, comfortable bed, Dr. Kim in Korea or Dick Wong in Hong Kong or Bailey Marks in Manila or Geoffrey Fletcher in Australia is sharing the plan of salvation with someone who may never have heard the Gospel unless God had given us the means to help with their support."

Witnessing, whether you're the sender or the sent, is simply sharing your faith in Jesus Christ. As a high school athlete returning from a camp with the Fellowship of Christian Athletes said, "I went there to see my `gods.' When I got there, I met their God. When I came home, their God was my God."

As a result of my experience in Arrowhead Springs, I was asked to serve on the international board of Campus Crusade, which I have done for over 20 years.

"History's Handful"

In 1975, I was also privileged to be part of what Bill Bright calls "History's Handful." To help carry the Gospel to Third World countries, Bill wanted to find 1,000 people to invest or raise $1,000,000 each. Since 1975 more than 300 people have committed to this program, and the money is being used strictly for evangelism and discipleship training.

Campus Crusade's emphasis on witnessing is one of the main reasons I am such a strong supporter of this program. I believe they reach more people at less cost per person than any other ministry I know.

Campus Crusade has 19,000 staff members and 281,000 trained volunteers in 172 countries, and "Jesus" (the film based on the life of Christ in the Gospel of Luke) has been translated into 454 languages. This film has been shown to millions of people in remote areas around the world by indigenous volunteers, who may be paid as little as 50 U.S. dollars a month. For many of the people seeing the film, it is their first time ever seeing a motion picture. According to records kept by Campus Crusade, one in every 10 people who see the film invite Christ to come into his or her life!

In the summer of 1990, before the Communist government collapsed, Ida and I went to the Soviet Union. We took with us *The Four Spiritual Laws* booklets printed in Russian. The people were amazed that I was giving them something printed in their own language, and they all seemed very appreciative.

I was so inspired and became so brave that I gave booklets to Russian soldiers and guards in the Hermitage. It wasn't until I returned to our ship that I began to think: "Our ship will be docked here for another day. What if the soldiers arrest me for distributing Christian literature? Suppose I am even executed?" I could imagine arriving in heaven and hearing St. Peter say, "You gave booklets to Russian soldiers? That was a dumb thing to do!" (Of course, Peter never would have said that!)

Soviet Diplomacy

Of course, nothing happened, and our ship went on to Poland, Finland, Latvia and Czechoslovakia. These countries had been under years of oppression, and there were many opportunities to share the Gospel, using *The Four Spiritual Laws* booklets translated into the appropriate languages.

Although my 1967 experience at Arrowhead Springs was a turning point, I have always been active in church. In fact, I have served as either a deacon or an elder since I was 25 years old.

One of the greatest pleasures of my life has been my association with Granada Presbyterian Church in Coral Gables. The church began as an outgrowth of the Shenandoah Presbyterian Church in Miami. A group of us living in Coral Gables began praying about building a church closer to home, on Granada Boulevard. In the early 1950s, when we received a tract of land as a gift from the Synod, the

Church Growth

local Presbyterian body of government, we built a small fellowship hall, approximately 40 by 80 feet.

Granada Presbyterian grew so quickly that, before long, we were holding Sunday School classes under the trees or on a sheltered porch. We needed more property, and several lots adjoining the church property were offered for sale. The congregation met and voted not to buy any additional property. So Bill McLeod, Joe Pyle, Selden Steward and I bought the land for the church's future use.

We soon needed those lots, and eventually we bought the entire block, as well as half a block across the street. Granada Presbyterian Church grew to over 1,000 members and became a very dynamic church.

To this day, the fellowship we enjoy in our home church is very important to us.

My deepening relationship with Christ didn't mean that I never struggled with forgiving others. In one case, a man wronged me by saying some untruths about me to defend his position. While I never confronted him about his actions, I could never bring myself to forgive him either.

> *When I can, I like to stand at the front door and welcome everyone to the Lord's house. This is perhaps the happiest time of my week, talking to these friends and giving them the recognition and attention they deserve as well as enjoy.*

Recently, after years of negative feelings, I invited him and his wife for lunch. We had a delightful time and talked for two hours. Afterward, I realized that I had not entertained a single negative thought about this man throughout our lunch together. God had removed my dislike for him and healed our relationship.

From the very beginning of my business life, community service has been important to me. I've always wanted to give something back to my community, to help make it a better place in which to live.

Over the years, I have served as a director or president of a number of community organizations. One of my favorite organizations was the Orange Bowl Committee. It is a group of Miami business leaders who work voluntarily to put on the New Year's Day football game and other events in December and January to attract tourists. Over the years, at one time or another, I worked on every committee and served as secretary, treasurer and vice president.

In connection with the Orange Bowl Game, I helped establish the annual Orange Bowl prayer breakfast. It remains a tremendously successful event, jointly sponsored by the Fellowship of Christian Athletes and the Orange Bowl Committee. In 1994, more than 2,000 high school students, business leaders and nationally famous sports figures attended. The sports figures shared their life-changing stories about their walk with Christ.

In 1969, I was elected president of the Orange Bowl Committee. I had a strong conviction that I wanted to honor God during my year as president, and I prayed that God would allow me to do this. I suggested to the committee that we invite Billy Graham to give the invocation before the game. However, the advisory council was afraid of offending television viewers and said, "No."

In December, out of the clear blue sky, I received a call from Billy Graham's assistant, Reverend T.W. Wilson. Billy Graham had just flown from a Southwest Conference football game with President Nixon on Air Force One. During their flight, the President told Billy he thought it would be good for the youth of America if Billy gave the invocation at a New Year's bowl game.

Rev. Wilson then called me and asked me if I would like to have Billy Graham give the invocation at the Orange Bowl Game. I went back to the advisory council, and they agreed that we couldn't turn down this opportunity. We extended an invitation to Billy Graham to pray at the Orange Bowl.

> *NBC reported that 62 million homes were tuned to the Orange Bowl. The following day, the Miami Herald published Billy Graham's prayer on the front page of the newspaper. I sat back and waited for the flood of complaints. Within a few days, I received two letters: one from a fan in the stadium who said his son was offended; another from a television viewer in Ohio. The other million letters never came.*

Before the pre-game activities, I told NBC's representative to make sure that Billy Graham's invocation was televised. He responded, "We're going to run a commercial instead. If we televise Billy Graham's prayer, people will change the channel. Or they will be so offended, they'll boycott our advertisers' products. Besides, we'd get millions of negative letters."

I had heard all these arguments before, but I was insistent. "If you don't have Billy Graham's prayer on television," I said, "I'll spend the rest of my life fighting your decision." The NBC repre-

Indicators
of a
Godly Life

*It is quite true that the way to live a godly life is not
an easy matter . . . . Be sure to use the abilities that God
has given you through His prophets when the elders of the
church laid their hands upon your head. Put these abilities to work; throw yourself into tasks so that everyone
may notice your improvement and progress. Keep a close
watch on all you do and think. Stay true to what is right
and God will bless you and use you to help others (I Timo-
thy 3:16; 4:14-16).*

I think the admonition, "Keep a close watch on all
you do and think," is one that can help us all be good
witnesses. We never know when someone is watching or
listening and may be affected by what we do or say. I often
pray that God will not let me offend Him by my actions.

The best way to witness is by the life we live. God and
other people will know our heart by these ten indicators
of a Christian witness. How do we:

1. React to frustration?
2. React to disappointments?
3. Serve the Lord?
4. Love the Lord?
5. Share our faith?
6. Accept victory?
7. Accept success?
8. Accept failure?
9. Spend our money?
10. Show love for one another?

sentative was really angry when he hastened to the control truck. Billy's invocation was televised in its entirety.

Going Back to Church

At the Allen Morris Company, I always encouraged my staff to participate in real estate organizations. Most of us faithfully attended local, state and national meetings.

In 1971, I inaugurated the first national prayer breakfast for the National Association of Realtors. The breakfast was held at the Fountainbleau Hotel on Miami Beach. Our featured speaker was Anita Bryant, the popular former Miss America who was famous for her television advertisements promoting Florida orange juice.

Everything went well — in the planning stages. However, we had guaranteed the hotel 1,000 people for breakfast on Sunday morning, and by Friday night, only 400 tickets had been sold. We were disappointed but committed the situation to God and promoted the event as best we could.

By Saturday, 800 tickets were sold. On Sunday morning, 1300 Realtors showed up, and several hundred people had to stand in the back. Anita Bryant gave a moving testimony about the miraculous survival of her twin babies, and there was hardly a dry eye in the room.

Afterwards, hundreds of Realtors told me how much they enjoyed the program. Many said, "I haven't been in church in years, and I'm going back!"

One week after this successful event, I was talking to Billy Graham on the phone. I said, "We had a great prayer breakfast at the Realtors' convention last week."

"Yes," he replied. "I know all about it. When are you going to have the next one?"

"Next November at the national convention."

Billy Graham asked where it would be. "Hawaii," I responded.

"I can be there," he said. I told him that I would like to get the Hula Bowl if he came, but he said the Coliseum would be big enough.

We were expecting 7,500 people, and all the arrangements went fine until October, when I made a routine check with the caterer whom I had employed on one of my three planning trips to Hawaii. "I can't do this breakfast," he said, surprising me. "There aren't enough coffee urns in the whole state of Hawaii to serve 7,500 people."

Four weeks to go, and I was without a caterer. I committed the situation to the Lord and went to see my friend, Dan Lui. Dan had retired as the police chief of Honolulu and was now vice president of American Airlines in the Pacific.

"Don't worry," Dan said. "American Airlines can cater the breakfast." He didn't even flinch as I ran through the menu: 7,000 orange juices, 6,000 Danish, 6,000 coffees, 1,000 milks and 1,000 teas. (I wondered what we would do with all the food if we didn't have a full house. However, that was no problem — the Coliseum was full, and all the food was eaten by guests.)

A few days before the breakfast date, Billy Graham told me that we should televise the breakfast so that all his friends on the islands could see the program. I made those arrangements, and his sermon was eventually shown on nationwide television as a public service of the National Association of Realtors.

Over the years, I have enjoyed serving on the boards of a number of colleges and seminaries, including Georgia Tech, Florida Presbyterian College, Montreat-Anderson College and Reformed Theological Seminary. My interest in education goes back to the

> *Helping someone with their seminary education is one of the best investments I can make to help multiply the Christian faith. When Reformed Theological Seminary trains someone for ministry, that one person may reach thousands of people for Christ during his or her lifetime.*

day my father told me that getting a college degree was the most important thing I could do.

I've been on the board of Reformed Theological Seminary in Jackson, Mississippi, for over 20 years. Six years ago, the seminary opened a branch in Orlando, Florida, and the enrollment has grown by a hundred students every year. In 1992, a third branch was opened in Charlotte, North Carolina.

Many of the students decide to come to seminary after they

are married and have a family. For many years, because the Allen Morris Foundation had been blessed with enough income to purchase some houses near the seminary, we made houses available rent-free to student families. Our plan was to provide for all major repairs and give paint to students who wanted to paint their houses.

The seminary recently purchased some apartments nearby, so the Foundation gave its houses to the seminary, enabling them to sell the houses and apply the proceeds to maintain the new apartments. The wonderful letters which we received over the years from those deserving students who lived in our houses were a strong encouragement to continue investing in young people.

The Night I Saw Jesus

Perhaps the reason I enjoy being sensitive to other people's needs is that Jesus Himself was sensitive to me and helped me in a time of great need.

I actually saw Jesus.

Ida and I were on the *Queen Elizabeth 2*, heading to Europe with George and Billy Akers in the summer of 1977, when I woke in the middle of the night, unable to move my arms or legs. I wanted to turn over, but I couldn't. I felt like I was paralyzed, and my first thought was that I had suffered a stroke.

I prayed. "Lord Jesus, I really need your help. If you want me to die, I'm ready, but please let me live until I get back to the United States. If I die on this ship, it will create all kinds of problems for my wife."

Then something happened which I will always treasure. As I looked out into the ocean, I saw Jesus walking across the water. He came right through the side of the ship and into my cabin. I don't remember whether He said anything, but He did hold out His hand and smile at me. Instantly I felt well, and I have never felt that good, before or since. Once again, I could move my arms and legs, and it seemed as if all my problems were over.

Because of my "deal" with God, I would not have been surprised to have a heart attack or stroke as soon as I returned to the United States. Fortunately, that didn't happen!

THE WORLD IN
1974

A hike in oil prices deepened a world-wide recession. In the United States, drivers routinely waited in long lines to buy gasoline, and President Richard Nixon imposed a nationwide 55-mile-an-hour speed limit for highway driving.

In August, President Nixon was forced to resign because of the "Watergate" scandal. In an effort to heal the wounds of the Vietnam war, President Gerald Ford extended a limited pardon to draft evaders, and peace returned to college campuses. The Symbionese Liberation Front kidnapped publishing heiress Patty Hearst.

In baseball, Hank Aaron hit his 715th career home run, breaking Babe Ruth's record. "Rhinestone Cowboy" and "The Way We Were" topped the record charts. Bob Woodward and Carl Bernstein wrote *All the President's Men*, and Aleksander Solzhenitsyn was expelled from the Soviet Union for publishing *The Gulag Archipelago*.

CHAPTER ELEVEN
Family Ties

By 1974, the Allen Morris Company was the largest developer of office structures in Florida. We had more than one million square feet of office rental space and were putting up a new building almost every month in Florida or Georgia.

With the company on solid footing, I focused less and less of my energies on business. A full 60 percent of my time was given to Christian and community activities and 10 percent to education.

It was then that an event occurred which reminded me of the importance of family and the love and commitment we share.

In 1974, our son Allen was a senior at Georgia Tech. At the same time, he was serving on our company and bank boards.

Allen was a pilot, and one evening, after returning from a day of board meetings in Miami, he rented a Piper Cherokee to fly six friends to a wedding in Houston. The group took off at 11:30 p.m. from Charlie Brown Airport in Atlanta. They had ascended to just 400 feet when the engine stopped. The plane was over a wooded residential area, and the only visible lights were from night traffic on I-20 and the "Six Flags" amusement park. Without enough speed or altitude to return to the airport, Allen decided to try gliding far enough to land on I-20.

The plane landed on the shoulder of the highway. It then crashed into a guardrail only a few feet from a 100-foot drop into

Crash Landing

the Chattahoochee River. The engine was severed from the fuselage and ended up on the highway, while the passengers and gas tanks remained on the shoulder.

A passing truck driver radioed for an ambulance, and Allen and his friends were taken to a hospital in Austell, Georgia.

Allen's roommate, Doug Faber, was driving home after dropping Allen at the airport, when he heard about the crash on his radio. He immediately drove to the hospital in Austell and then called me at 1 a.m. "They are all alive and seem okay," said Doug. "The hospital is so overcrowded that Allen is in the maternity ward!"

When I arrived at the hospital, Allen was asleep. Because of the shortage of hospital help, no one had washed his face, and he still had matted blood in his hair. His body was covered by a sheet, with his feet sticking out at the bottom.

Ida decided to stay at home and pray while I caught the 3 a.m. flight to Atlanta. "I dedicated Allen to the Lord when he was a little boy," she said. "He's in the Lord's hands now."

The doctors had told me that Allen had a back injury. As I looked at him lying motionless on the hospital bed, I was afraid that he was paralyzed. Finally, I got up enough nerve to touch his toe, and he moved his foot. I felt a tremendous sense of relief and gratitude to God.

One week later, after fitting him with a back brace, the hospital released Allen. They told him that he had a strained back, but I was totally unaware that he was in excruciating pain.

On our way to Jim and Ida Bell's home in Atlanta, Allen asked me to stop by the shop where the back brace was made, to have it fitted. The manager there took one look at Allen and said, "Son, you have a broken back!" He adjusted the brace and told us to see another doctor. We were both shocked. Why would the hospital in Austell release Allen if he had a broken back?

At Jim and Ida's, Allen went to take a shower. A few minutes later, I heard a shout from the bathroom, "Dad!" I rushed in just in time for Allen to collapse into my arms.

I immediately drove Allen to Piedmont Hospital. A specialist there told us that Allen had a serious back injury which would require spinal fusion surgery and could take as long as a year to heal. We discussed several options for doctors and hospitals and decided upon Doctors' Hospital, just a few blocks from our home in Coral Gables.

In Coral Gables, the doctors informed us that they would have to operate on Allen's back to fuse his broken vertebrae. With or without the operation, it was possible that he would be paralyzed. It was also expected that Allen would never be able to have children. One doctor told me, "This operation is so dangerous that if Allen were my son, I wouldn't let him have it."

I explained all this to Allen. He still wanted to go ahead. The first two operations failed. The third operation lasted eight hours...and was successful!

When Allen regained consciousness, I asked him if there was anything I could do for him. "Yes," he said. "I want you to memorize Philippians 4:6-7." The next time I saw him, I recited: "Be anxious for nothing, but in everything by prayer and supplication, let your requests be made known to God."
"You left out the most important part," said Allen. "By prayer and supplication with thanksgiving!"
I was extremely moved. Here was my son, who didn't know whether or not he would ever walk again, reminding me to pray "with thanksgiving." I felt like I grew more spiritually in those few minutes than I had in my entire Christian life.

Allen still had to spend many months in the hospital. To help him keep up his spirits, he asked me to come every morning and read to him from Psalms and Proverbs.

I agreed. Early every morning, I arrived in Allen's room and read out loud from the Bible. Often, he was still asleep when I began, and he woke up while I was reading.

It was the first time in my life that I took the time for daily Bible reading, and these weeks were a tremendous blessing for me. I learned to praise the Lord, regardless of my circumstances, and I came to understand the truth of Romans 8:28: "And we know that in all things God works for the good of those who love Him, who have been called according to His purpose."

Allen discusses our time together:

> My airplane crash was one of the most terrible, painful and beautiful experiences of my life. After one of the failed operations, my partial paralysis became total paralysis. I had to mentally prepare for the possibility of life in a wheelchair.
>
> The Lord used this time to give me a new empathy for others in pain and with handicaps. I also realized that I was mortal and felt a deep desire to make my life count — for however many months or years the Lord would give me.
>
> One unexpected benefit of my accident was the chance to develop a new relationship with my father. He was not around much when I was growing up, and at 13 I had left home for McCallie School. I knew how busy he was, and now I could hardly believe it when he began taking the time to come to the hospital, to read the Bible and pray with me every morning. It was a precious time for us, a time to get to know one another and an opportunity for me to appreciate him as my father and as my treasured friend.

During the months that Allen stayed in the hospital, his mother and I visited him every day. I never once heard a word of complaint. He spent a great deal of time in a stryker-frame bed, unable to turn over. For meals, he was strapped down, then attendants flipped him *and* the bed over, so that he could eat through a hole in the top of the bed. He did not know whether he would ever walk again, but he was always cheerful and never asked, "Why me?"

Today, we continue to praise and thank God for Allen's miraculous healing, his beautiful wife and their four precious children.

Learning Obedience

After nine months in a body cast and three months in a back brace, Allen recovered completely — but not before I had time to reflect on my relationship with my children.One of the few regrets of my life is how little time I spent with them while they were growing up. It was only later that I learned one of the most important ways I could serve God was at home, loving and caring for my family.

Despite my oversight, all our children turned out well, thanks to Ida's hard work and loving example. In fact, I don't know how they could have turned out any better, and today we are a close-knit family.

One day, Ida asked Allen if he was learning patience. He replied, "No, Mother, I am learning obedience to God. I know that He does not allow a single mistake, and I just hope I don't miss any lessons that He is trying to teach me through this."

A passage in the Bible that has greatly influenced my behavior and character is Exodus 20:5: ". . . For I, the Lord your God, am a jealous God, punishing the children for the sins of the fathers to the third and fourth generation of those who hate me, but showing love to a thousand generations of those who love me and keep my commandments." I never wanted to cause trouble for my children or grandchildren or any future generations by my lack of obedience to God and His laws. I always felt that if I lived a moral life and did the right things, my family would benefit.

Over the years, it is Ida's strength and Christian commitment that have held our family together. I love my wife. In fact, our relationship and my love for her are central to my life. I couldn't live with myself if she didn't respect my morals, my commitment to Christ and my business ethics. She has been a wonderful wife and sweetheart, a superb mother and a loving grandmother. She is a much better person than I am, and I often wonder how I was so blessed to have her in my life.

Wife, Mother, Grandmother and Sweetheart

Ida's salvation experience was a great event in our lives, and she has had more influence on me than any other person. She always has shown confidence in anything I attempt to do. When I decided to start my own business, young Ida was heading to college, Kay was in junior high, and Allen was in elementary school. We had a mortgage on our home. Yet, as usual, Ida demonstrated full confidence in my decision to step out on my own.

We have been married 55 years, and we still tell each other, "I love you," all the time. We say it first thing every morning, and it is the last thing we say to each other before we go to sleep. My only regret is that, since Ida is most likely to outlive me, I won't always be around to take care of her. I know the Lord will do it, but in the meantime, I am glad He uses me.

As a businessman and father, I wanted my children to know the value of hard work. I didn't want us to live ostentatiously. In my mind, "rich people" were aloof and uncaring, like the people on my paper route, when I was 12, who only let me talk to the servants when I came to collect my money. Although I had become successful in business, I was always aware that I was just an ordinary person with a lot of undeserved blessings, and I wanted my children to feel the same way.

In 1955, I established the Allen Morris Foundation to handle most of my charitable giving. I had a great desire to help disadvantaged people and deserving organizations, and I wanted to give in a more intelligent way.

However, one of my most compelling reasons for establishing the foundation was so that I could train my children to give away money. The first time I gave money away, it was incredibly difficult, and I really didn't know if I could do it. Eventually, I overcame my reluctance, but I didn't want my children to have such a hard time.

Today, all our companies tithe their income to the Allen Morris Foundation. This is a predetermined decision and requires no action by the board or company officers. The Foundation meets regularly and gives most of its

Lessons in Giving

funds to people who are sharing God's love and telling others how they can have a personal relationship with Christ. We support missionaries and other people in full-time Christian service. One of our most rewarding ministries is the "Executive Ministries Outreach," which is specifically directed toward business and professional leaders and their spouses. We host breakfasts, luncheons and executive dinners so that others can hear the life stories of outstanding leaders whose lives have been changed through a personal relationship with Jesus Christ.

"You don't use money as much as money uses you." It's a true statement: if a person has money, he or she is responsible for spending and investing it properly.

Giving away money is actually a tough job, because it is hard to decide who needs help the most. I have Scottish blood in me, so I can't stand throwing money away or paying more for something than it is worth. Giving money away with God's purposes in mind, however, is an investment.

Giving: A Tough, Important Job

It sounds strange, but I like to make money so I can give it away! I won't go to the horse races and bet $2 on a horse, because I know that this money can go a long way toward building God's kingdom on earth. Two dollars will buy 20 *Four Spiritual Laws* booklets, and there is no telling how many people could come to Christ through those 20 little booklets.

In the fall of 1965, a very special young man entered our lives, Edward (Eddie) Paul Waxer. He was a recent graduate of the University of Michigan and on staff with Campus Crusade for Christ at the University of Miami campus.

Eddie has been a tremendous blessing to our family in many ways, including his friendship. His most unforgettable, eternal gift was leading our son-in-law, Jim, and each of our children into an understanding of God's plan of salvation. Jim was 26, Ida, 24, Kay, 21, and Allen, 13, when they each surrendered their lives to Jesus. This, of course, is the greatest of God's gifts, and all of us will be forever grateful to Eddie for this.

The Greatest Gift

Eddie has progressed in his ministry and today is the founder and president of World Sports. He recruits leading athletes, in major sports worldwide, to share their faith in Jesus Christ. In this way, his ministry impacts many thousands of lives throughout the world.

He and his wife, Patt, are an integral part of our family, and we love them very much.

The following four principles will help you discover how to know God personally and experience the abundant life He promised.

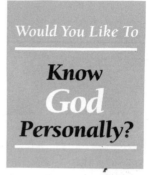

Would You Like To

Know

God

Personally?

God **loves** you and created you to know Him personally.
(References contained in this booklet should be read in context from the Bible whenever possible.)

God's Love

"God so loved the world that He gave His one and only Son, that whoever believes in Him shall not perish but have eternal life" (John 3:16).

God's Plan

"This is eternal life: that they may know you, the only true God, and Jesus Christ, whom you have sent" (John 17:3, NIV).

What prevents us from knowing God personally?

Man is **sinful** and **separated** from God, so we cannot know Him personally or experience His love.

Man Is Sinful

Man was created to have fellowship with God; but, because of his own stubborn self-will, he chose to go his own independent way, and fellowship with God was broken. This self-will, characterized by an attitude of active rebellion or passive indifference, is an evidence of what the Bible calls sin.

\ **Holy God** /

Man Is Separated

"The wages of sin is death" [spiritual separation from God] (Romans 6:23).

This diagram illustrates that God is holy and man is sinful. A great gulf separates the two. The arrows illustrate that man is continually trying to reach God and establish a personal relationship with Him through his own efforts, such as a good life, philosophy, or religion — but he enevitably fails.

/ **Sinful Man** \

The third principle explains the only way to bridge this gulf...

Jesus Christ is God's **only** provision for man's sin. Through Him alone we can know God personally and experience God's love.

He Died In Our Place

"God demonstrates His own love for us in this: While we were still sinners, Christ died for us" (Romans 5:8).

He Rose From The Dead

"Christ died for our sins . . . He was buried . . . He was raised on the third day according to the Scriptures . . . He appeared to Peter, and then to the twelve. After that, He appeared to more than five hundred . . ." (I Corinthians 15:3-6).

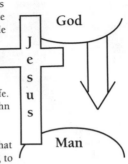

He Is The Only Way To God

"Jesus answered, 'I am the way and the truth and the life. No one comes to the Father except through me' " (John 14:6).

This diagram illustrates that God has bridged the gulf that separates us from Him by sending His Son, Jesus Christ, to die on the cross in our place to pay the penalty for our sins.

It is not enough just to know these truths . . .

4

We must individually **receive** Jesus Christ as Savior and Lord; then we can know God personally and experience His love.

We Must Receive Christ

"As many as received Him, to them He gave the right to become children of God, even those who believe in His name" (John 1:12).

We Receive Christ Through Faith

"By grace you have been saved through faith; and that not of yourselves, it is the gift of God; not as a result of works that no one should boast" (Ephesians 2:8, 9).

When We Receive Christ, We Experience A New Birth.
We Receive Christ By Personal Invitation

[Christ speaking] "Behold, I stand at the door and knock; if anyone hears My voice and opens the door, I will come in to him." (Revelation 3:20).

Receiving Christ involves turning to God from self (repentence) and trusting Christ to come into our lives to forgive us of our sins and to make us what He wants us to be. Just to agree intellectually that Jesus Christ is the Son of God and that He died on the cross for our sins is not enough. Nor is it enough to have an emotional experience. We receive Jesus Christ by faith, as an act of our will.

You Can Receive Christ Right Now By Faith Through Prayer

(Prayer is talking with God)

God knows your heart and is not so concerned with your words as He is with the attitude of your heart. The following is a suggested prayer:

> *"Lord Jesus, I want to know You personally. Thank You for dying on the cross for my sins. I open the door of my life and receive You as my Savior and Lord. Thank You for forgiving my sins and giving me eternal life. Take control of the throne of my life. Make me the kind of person you want me to be."*

Does this prayer express the desire of your heart?

If it does, pray this prayer right now, and Christ will come into your life, as He promised.

THE WORLD IN THE
1980s

It was a decade that began with Jimmy Carter in the White House and American hostages in Iran. In Poland, Lech Walensa founded the first labor movement in a Soviet Bloc country, and serious, widespread dissent began to appear among other Soviet satellites. In China, a lone student stood motionless in front of an approaching tank, bearing witness to the yearning for freedom sweeping totalitarian countries.

In the United States, an ex-Hollywood actor, Ronald Reagan, was elected to two terms as President. A deep recession gave way to a period of prosperity and overspending, and by 1985, the United States was a debtor nation for the first time in seventy years. In 1986, the country mourned the deaths of five astronauts aboard the space shuttle, *Challenger*.

Meanwhile, "hippies" grew into "yuppies," and personal computers and microwave ovens became common household items. While families cocooned at home with rented movies and VCRs, a renaissance on Broadway produced a series of remarkable plays: *Dream Girls, Les Miserables* and *Phantom of the Opera*.

CHAPTER TWELVE
The Secrets of Success

By 1980, the Allen Morris Company had completed its 67th building in Florida, and I was ready to turn the day-to-day running of the company over to my son, Allen. Allen was then 27, and he had worked for the company over a period of 10 years.

When Allen took over the Allen Morris Company, I decided to concentrate my efforts on managing the family's liquid assets. Real estate investors agree that "there is nothing liquid about real estate," and we diversified among six mutual funds and employed several highly successful advisers.

Staying the Course

One of Ken Keyes favorite sayings was "Give to the world the best you have, and the best will come back to you." It was a saying I first learned from my second grade teacher, Mrs. Cloud, and I found it to be true all my life.

I could have retired when I was 40, and I considered doing so and going to seminary. Later, I concluded that, since I was so successful in making money and enjoyed giving it away to the Lord's work, it was best for me to keep using my talents in the business world.

Looking back, I can see that there were many contributing factors to the success I enjoyed. I tried to seek the will of God and maintain high ethical standards, as well as to seek guidance from others. I also learned a great deal about negotiating, dealing with employees and handling setbacks.

When people ask my advice about starting a business, I try to determine why they have chosen that particular business and why they think it will be successful. I in-

Starting a Business: Some Important Questions

quire about their education and experience and then ask them the following questions:

> •Is having your own business one of the most important things in your life?
> •Are you ready to work hard, to do menial tasks and not go home until your work is done?
> •Are you willing to sacrifice some of the recreational activities in which you normally participate? Are you willing to make your clothes and your car last another year?
> •Is your wife or husband also willing?

The bottom line in starting a business is: If you are willing to apply yourself to getting the job done, the result will most likely be success.

There was a time in my life when I made a lot of fast decisions, without even thinking about talking them over with the Lord. Today, I am in constant communication with God, trying to learn and follow His will. I pray perhaps a dozen times a day, asking God for guidance and thanking him for his many blessings.

In making decisions, I of-

Partners with God

ten use a process of elimination. I think of all the numerous possibilities and then ask myself, "What would be pleasing to God?" In this way, I am forced to completely subordinate myself to God's will.

Above all, I have a feeling of great confidence in God's omnipotence. I know that He knows what is best in every situation, and that He can make good things happen.

God has kept me out of deals, too. More than once I have

worked hard on a deal that didn't happen, only to find out, years later, how lucky I was that it didn't go through.

For example, I tried to lease a tract of land across the street from the 1000 Brickell Building at a time when the land was cheap. We wanted to negotiate a 99-year lease. The lawyers made some additions to the lease that I couldn't accept, and eventually someone else signed the lease and built a large office building on the site.

Closed Doors

At the time, I felt discouraged. However, the company that put up the building had trouble getting tenants because several other office buildings were constructed at the same time. If the Allen Morris Company had made the lease and put up a building, we would have ended up in the same trouble. In hindsight, I'm glad God kept me from that deal!

I have never believed that wealth was a sign of God's blessing. Some of the happiest people I know have limited incomes, and there are many millionaires with no concern for other people. In fact, plenty of people make their money by preying on the weaknesses of their fellow man.

I never wanted to make my money in companies that produced cigarettes or alcohol, and I do not invest in those kinds of companies. I wouldn't get any pleasure out of making a big profit from a company whose business is appealing to the weakness of other human beings.

Success in business is absolutely meaningless without honesty and fairness. The truth is that people are either honest or dishonest; they cannot be "almost honest." Over the years, at the Allen Morris Company we have had to encourage some people to leave because they misrepresented the facts.

A Question of Honesty . . .

In all our building projects, none of the building inspectors have ever asked for a bribe. I know they ask a lot of other people, but they never asked me — and I consider that a compliment.

We were negotiating for a building project in a foreign country, and after six months of hard work, we had advanced all the way to the man who would take the paper in for the president's signature. The man and I met to work out the last minute details, but after I left the room, he asked my lawyer, "What's in it for me?" That was the end of the deal.

In 1967, I was offered an opportunity to buy a half interest in the Miami Dolphins. The deal presented tremendous tax advantages, the bank was willing to lend me the money, and my legal and accounting advisors all strongly recommended going forward.

. . . and Conscience

As the time for a decision grew closer, I found that my conscience was bothering me because the Miami Dolphins played their games on Sunday. Although I didn't believe it was wrong to watch games on the Sabbath, it didn't seem right to participate in providing that kind of entertainment for others.

The feeling became so strong that I had to terminate our negotiations. I don't feel critical of others who own professional athletic teams, but I felt that part of my commitment to Christ was to obey his precepts. This included the commandment to honor the Sabbath (Exodus 20:8-11).

An important key to financial success is making wise investments, and the key to investing is "compound interest." This is a concept that many people do not understand, but it isn't all that difficult.

If you invest money at 10 percent and reinvest your profits every year, this

Wise Investments and Compound Interest

is called "compounding your money." At 10 percent a year, if you leave the money in for 7.2 years, the investment will double. At 20 percent a year, it takes only three and a half years to double your money — but you can't spend any of it. In almost every case, I reinvest the profits of my investments so they will compound.

When I was growing up, a neighbor boy convinced me to trade my .410 shotgun for his nine-foot fishing rod. I seldom used the fishing rod, I missed my gun, and I knew I got the worst end of the deal. Since then, I have been a much more careful negotiator.

The key to successful negotiation is finding out what the other party wants. If you can get them to tell you where they are willing to start and what they are willing to do, you have the beginnings of a successful negotiation.

Back to School

Although I consider myself a good negotiator, there are times when I have lessons of my own to learn. Our negotiations for the Northside Shopping Center finally came down to one $100,000 item, for which I thought the buyer should pay. The buyer refused, and we argued over it for a half hour or more. A hundred thousand dollars is a lot of money, but relative to the agreed-upon price, it was not a large percentage.

Finally, my lawyer, Doug Batchelor, suggested that we take a break. In private, he asked me, "Do you want to sell this shopping center?"

"Of course I do!"

"Well," Doug responded. "You're about to sell it for $12 million. Do you really want to hold things up for $100,000?"

I did want that money, but I didn't want to lose the deal, so I agreed with Doug. The point is that businessmen really do need good lawyers to keep them from making foolish mistakes!

Like any successful business person, I have had many people who helped me along the way. Arthur Vining Davis, for example, was not only a great friend but a mentor. He was a man I wanted to emulate because he was honest, fair, genuine and considerate of others. He not only liked people but wanted to be liked by them. This was also a basic trait of my personality. In fact, throughout

Guides Along the Way

my career, I have often thought of the words of Will Rogers, "I never met a person I didn't like."

I remember one conversation I had with Mr. Davis on an airplane. He always was reading more than one book at a time, and I asked him, "If you had to do it over again, what would you study in college?"

"Liberal arts," he responded. "This background prepares one to appreciate literature and art to the fullest!"

Another man from whom I learned a great deal was Grady Harris, my lawyer and friend. He was known for his highly ethical and professional behavior, and I always consulted him on company business. At one closing, the client's attorney, Stuart Patton, asked me who had drawn up the papers. When I said, "Grady Harris," he turned to the signature page and, without even reading the rest of the document, told his client, "You can sign here." I thought that was the highest compliment one lawyer could pay another.

Knowing that so many people had helped me in my business career, I wanted to help others. For example, one young man who came to work for me early in his career was Bill Spencer, an accountant. I had invested in a pest control company in Atlanta that was doing poorly, and Bill agreed to see what he could do to improve the situation. While still supervising his accounting staff in Miami, he turned around the company in Atlanta.

Finally, Bill told me, "I think I need to live in Atlanta to run the company properly." Because he had earned it, I sold the company to him for one dollar. Not surprisingly, Bill is very successful now — and his family loves Atlanta.

As a businessman, I always have considered it important to treat employees with appreciation and respect and to compensate them fairly. I also like to call attention to their successes.

When employees make mistakes, it is important to understand why. They may have been given a job beyond their capability. If an employee isn't qualified for a job, they can probably be trained. If an employee makes a mistake of discretion by revealing company projects to a competitor, they can learn to be more careful. Of course, if information is shared deliberately, that's not a mistake but a betrayal.

Honest people can make honest mistakes, and it is essential that employees have room to learn and grow from their own experiences.

At the Allen Morris Company, I have tried to create a positive atmosphere and maintain high professional standards. As far as I know, our employees enjoy their jobs. I feel fatherly toward them and would like to think that they feel free to share their problems with me.

God has sent people to the Allen Morris Company whom I didn't look for and didn't think I needed.

Twenty years ago, a young man came to me and said, "I want

to work for you. I can do the things that you need done, so that you won't have to do them yourself."

"I like the things I do," I responded, "and I don't want you to do them for me."

Persistence Pays Off

He was persistent, and eventually I had to come right out and tell him that I didn't want him to work for me. Then he offered to work for nothing.

"You can't do that," I said. "Your family needs you to take care of them."

He replied, "If you let me work for you, whatever you pay me will be all right."

I agreed and told him that I would compensate him according to his worth for the company. The first month I paid him around $800. As time went by, I gave him a little interest in the projects on which he was working.

The young man worked for me for 10 years. When he left, I bought the interests we had given him in various projects for two million dollars!

Like all businessmen, I have had my share of disappointment. During the October, 1987, stock crash, the Allen Morris Company lost about a half-million dollars of our stock values. My first thought was, "I could have given those profits to the Lord's work. Now, they have disappeared."

The October crash affected all our business dealings. It was the most disastrous day in American stocks since the crash of 1929. Thousands of people had their investments wiped out overnight.

A Lesson from the 1987 Crash

In handling these disappointment, I learned a lesson from Albert Huddleston, who is the son-in-law of Texas millionaire Bunker Hunt. Several years ago, Huddleston lost his fortune in silver speculation. A year before the silver crash, he had given $1,000,000 to Campus Crusade. "I'm so glad I gave that money away," he said. "Otherwise, I would have lost it, too."

In times of financial setbacks, it helps me to reflect on the words of Jesus:

*"Do not lay up for yourselves treasures on earth,
where moth and rust destroy and where thieves break in
and steal; but lay up for yourselves treasures in heaven,
where neither moth nor rust destroys and where thieves
do not break in and steal. For where your treasure is,
there your heart will be also."*

Matthew 6:19-21

"Excessive profits breed ruinous competition." It is an important axiom that I learned at a real estate seminar, and it is the reason I have always wanted to be the low bidder.

When I bid competitively on buildings with long-term leases, I figured my costs as closely as possible. If I charged just enough rent to properly clean, repair and air condition the building, with enough cushion to pay the mortgage, I usually won the contract. Under this plan, my profits came in 15 or 20 years down the road, when the mortgage was paid off.

Successful Business Strategy

This strategy worked for some time — until the unexpected occurred. Over the years, the Allen Morris Company had constructed a number of buildings for Southern Bell, leasing them to the company for 10 to 15 year terms. With the breakup of AT&T, Southern Bell no longer needed these buildings. Most of them were "one purpose" buildings, constructed to Southern Bell's specifications and located in prime locations particularly suited to their needs.

All at once, the Allen Morris Company found itself with a half-dozen vacant buildings, totaling nearly 250,000 square feet. Our normal yearly rental income from these buildings had produced a profit. Now, we were without enough income to cover maintenance, insurance, taxes and mortgage payments.

All of these changes came about in a three-year period, at a time when office buildings were overbuilt. There were vacancies everywhere, and we were unable to find tenants for much of this space. Our substantial income was converted to heavy expenses, and even now this situation is just beginning to turn around.

The business strategy that seems to make the most sense now is to buy undervalued assets, like office buildings, which have intrinsic value but which are unpopular for other investors. I have always liked the long-term business strategy attributed to Baron de Rothschild: "I always want to accommodate the public. When the public wants to sell, I'll buy. When the public wants to buy, I'll sell!"

Following is an excerpt from a letter I wrote to my son, W. Allen, on July 10, 1978.

Now, the head of a business must plan for to-morrow — and the day after, and the years ahead. He must be aware of what can be done if a substantial source of income is lost.

Passing the Baton

He must have a plan to protect his key and valued employees in bad times and good. Although you cannot expect or count on loyalty from your employees, they expect and count on loyalty from you.

That's why it is important to always consider what job a particular person might fill if his present job should disappear. It's also important to maintain reserves in the company, so key people can be retained in bad times.

Most employees look only at the present. They say, "How much money can I make today?" They aren't thinking about security; they only want to know, "Why can't the company pay out more of its profits?"

Yes, those are the questions they ask, and I believe for the most part they are sincere. But when times change, they expect the company to look after them and their families.

I think it is far more important to support good people in bad times than it is to overpay them in good times and then let them go, as some do, when the going gets tough.

When we had the big real estate recession in the fall of 1974, we had to let only one person go — and we did not let him go until we helped him find another job.

You must guard against giving anyone too much

power or authority beyond that needed to administer and perform the work assigned to him.

Many people say they like an executive who can make a quick decision. I belong to the group that likes to see an executive take the time he needs to make a sound decision.

I think one of the things that helped me most in my business career was having someone with whom I could discuss other people and issues on a confidential basis. However, remember, no matter how much advice you get, when the decision is finally made, the one making it has all the responsibility.

One of the points I have always emphasized in my talks on sales has been discernment. Your success will depend to a great degree on how you discern what is most important and what is least important. A man, no matter what his job — ditch digger, farmer, salesman, President of the United States — must discern on a daily or hourly basis what is the most important thing for him to do next.

Finally, it is important to be flexible. Many people fail because they set their course and continue on it regardless of what the radar tells them. Think flexible, discern what's most important — and do it!

THE WORLD IN THE
1990s

In the shadow of the third millennium, old conflicts erupted into war. With full television coverage from Ted Turner's CNN, the United States defeated Iraq in "Operation Desert Storm." War broke out in former Yugoslavia, and Islamic fundamentalists bombed the World Trade Center in New York.

At the same time, there were inspiring moments of peace and hope. The totalitarian empire of the Soviet Union disintegrated almost overnight. East and West Germans danced on the crumbling Berlin Wall, and apartheid ended in South Africa. New peace initiatives began in Ireland and the Middle East.

In the United States, Hurricane Andrew devastated South Florida, and the Mississippi River flooded eight midwestern states. On Broadway, there was a revival of popular show tunes, including *Carousel* and *Showboat*. The enduringly popular *Gone with the Wind* spawned a television mini-series, and the revolution in communications continued with the advent of fax machines, e-mail and pocket telephones.

CHAPTER THIRTEEN
Enduring Legacy

I am now in my eighties, and the dateline of the world is rapidly moving toward the year 2000. My life has spanned most of the twentieth century, and I am amazed at the enormous changes that have taken place in the world during this time.

I don't know what God's plan is for my future. It may be life, or it may be life's end. I don't try to figure these things out; instead, I try to do my best every day to honor Him, to do the job He has given me to do.

In a recent Sunday school class, we discussed the second coming of Jesus. This has never been a problem for me. I feel that I want to be in fellowship with Him at all times, loving, honoring and serving Him. When He comes again and calls me home, I'll be ready.

> *Over the years, I have often prayed, "What can I do for you, Lord?"*

God has constantly shown me new ways to serve Him and given me the strength to do what He asks. It has been one of the most exciting parts of my life.

I am so grateful for the way the Lord has blessed our family and protected us over the years. When I think of the world in which my grandchildren and their children will grow up, I sometimes feel afraid. Yet I know that God is faithful to each generation and that He will take care of them just as He has cared for us.

Have you experienced the great joy of seeing God's goodness flow through one person's life to another? I see it in Ida's life almost daily. As a Christian, she loves everyone and wants only the best for them.

My Prayer for You

You can have this wonderful experience yourself. God's plan of salvation is yours for the asking.

The prayer that Paul wrote from his cell in a Roman prison to his Christian brothers and sisters in Ephesus is my prayer for you:

> *"And I pray that Christ will be more and more at home in your hearts, living within you as you trust in Him. May your roots go down deep into the soil of God's marvelous love; and may you be able to feel and understand, as all God's children should, how long, how wide, how deep, and how high His love really is; and to experience this love for yourselves, though it is so great that you will never see the end of it or fully know or understand it. And so at last you will be filled up with God Himself."*
>
> *Ephesians 3:17-19*

Today, almost all my thoughts and prayers are for a better world for my children and grandchildren. I really want them to have lives that are happy and give glory to God. Ida and I are tremendously blessed by the fact that all our children and grandchildren love the Lord and have a personal relationship with Jesus Christ. I love each of them so very much.

Over the years, I have discovered that it is not money or "things" that make life satisfying. Instead, a good life is the result of a grateful attitude for what we have. Although it is difficult to give advice to people, if I could pass on any wisdom to my grandchildren and their descendants, it would be the following thoughts, always keeping in mind honesty and loyalty.

Several years ago, Ida put her faith into action through a prison ministry in South Florida. The results have been immeasurable. She recounts the experience:

> Sometime ago, the chaplain of the Dade County Correctional System asked me if I would serve on the board of his prison ministry. About the same time,

the president of Montreat-Anderson asked me to serve on the college board. I was in my seventies and was extremely surprised at their invitations. Because I didn't want to serve on either board, I put both requests out of my mind.

Behind Bars

When I finally realized I was being rude by not responding, I asked God to show me what to do. Although I know this is not the way we are supposed to seek God's guidance, I decided to open my Bible and read the first thing I saw there.

My Bible fell open to the story of Jonah. I said, "Oh, Lord, don't tell me this! I don't want to do either one of these jobs." The next morning, I called up both men and told them I needed to be on their board.

I didn't think I should serve on the board of a jail ministry without knowing what happened in the jail, so I decided to visit there. That was the Lord's way of getting me into prison ministry! Today, I am no longer on the ministry board, but I still go to jail every Wednesday.

With several friends from church, I arrive at the Dade County Women's Shelter around eight o'clock in the morning. After searching our bags and taking our keys and pocketbooks, the guards allow us into the dining room. Here, we conduct a Bible study and talk with the inmates about their problems. Sometimes, we have as many as forty women. We give each woman a Gideon Bible, as well as Christian literature and magazines.

People who don't do this kind of work might think that a great gulf exists between the inmates and me. Just the opposite is true. I am always aware that, except for the grace of God, I could be in jail, too.

I try to help the women see the Lord's sovereignty in all that has happened. Sometimes, I ask, "Do you know why you are in jail?" The women usually mention drug use or some other crime. I tell them, "No, you are here because the Lord wants to draw you closer to Him. You will probably never again have so much time for praying and studying the Word. Take advantage of this time to know Him better."

Many inmates are responsive to this message, because so many have known the Lord or have had a mother or grandmother that prayed for them. They have fallen away from doing what they know is right, but they have an excitement about learning to serve the Lord.

It is such a blessing for me to be there in the prison, and I often thank the women for letting me come talk with them. Like any teacher, I get more out of the lesson than my students. The other church people with whom I work feel the same way. When we leave the jail, we are on cloud nine. It is the joy and exhilaration that comes from knowing you are doing God's will and that you are a part of His work in the world.

These days, it seems like Ida and I are as busy as we were in the first few years of our marriage. I am particularly proud of Ida's jail ministry, which she has been involved in for more than ten years.

I still feel very responsible for telling my friends and acquaintances about Christ. When people accept Jesus as their Savior, they have life everlasting and go to heaven when they

The Final Word

die. If they don't accept Jesus, they are separated from God for all of eternity. I didn't make the rules; I just read the Bible. But I believe what Scripture says, and that is why I'm so anxious for my friends to accept Christ as Lord.

On January 28, 1998, a few weeks after his 84th birthday, L. Allen Morris went home to be with the Lord.

Nuggets of Wisdom
from L. Allen Morris

About Learning
- Reading is important.
- College is important.
- Never stop learning.
- Always search for new ways to do old things.
- Be a good listener. It's amazing how much you can learn by listening to other people about their jobs or favorite subjects.

About People
- You can't have too many friends.
- Look for a mentor to challenge and encourage you.
- Observe positive and negative traits in people to emulate or avoid their character qualities.

About Business Life
- Always give your best to your job.
- Be trustworthy.
- Be reliable.
- Be there when you are needed.
- Be interested in your associates and their families.

About Family Life
- Love your family in every way.

About Christian Life
- Read and obey the Ten Commandments (Exodus 20).
- Remember, without the Lord, life will be frustrating and empty.

About Dreams
- Don't be afraid to dream a little.
- Lay your hopes and dreams before the Lord and follow his leading.
- *Without a vision, the people perish. . . .*

Proverbs 29:18

Inspirational Thoughts
from Ida Akers Morris

Prayer for the Joyful Life
My prayer for each of you is for a life characterized by:

- A deep love for the Lord and acceptance of Him as Lord and Savior;
- Gratefulness for all the Lord has given you;
- Joy running so deep that others can see it;
- Acceptance of whatever circumstances the Lord sends your way, the bad as well as the good;
- An awareness that God is in control of every area of your life, and the indescribable peace which comes with this knowledge;
- Forgiveness for yourself and others, as well as patience, remembering that God always forgives and is not finished with any of us yet.

Who shall separate us from the love of Christ? Shall trouble or hardship or persecution or famine or nakedness or danger or sword? As it is written: For your sake we face death all day long; we are considered as sheep to be slaughtered.

No, in all these things we are more than conquerors through Him who loved us. For I am convinced that neither death nor life, neither angels nor demons, neither the present nor the future, nor any powers, neither height nor depth, nor anything else in all creation, will be able to separate us from the love of God that is in Christ Jesus our Lord.

Romans 8:35-39.

THE THIRD GENERATION
Allen Morris' Grandchildren Share
the Wisdom He Passed to Them

At Thanksgiving two months before he died, my grandfather and I sat down and he opened his Bible to the book of Exodus, Chapter 20, Verses 5 and 6 and he read:

> For I, the Lord your God, am a jealous God, punishing the children for the sin of their fathers to the third and fourth generation of those who hate me, but showing love to a thousand generations of those who love me and keep my commandments.

He told me that when he learned this verse, he realized that his decision to love the Lord and follow His commandments would not only effect his life, but also the lives of his children and grandchildren.

Katie Bell, 23

Pulling weeds, going to Sears, buying boxes of doughnuts. Of all the memories and wisdom of my grandfather, L. Allen Morris — we called him "BD," short for "Big Daddy" — I will never forget his challenge to me in my early adolescence. It was a Saturday morning, we were alone in one of his heavy steel automobiles heading toward a hotel exhibit half full of rows of old used shotguns and the smell of gun oil, pipe tobacco, concession stand popcorn, and the occasional stinky cigar. As the big car rolled down the road, BD said in a very serious, gentle, but direct way, "You know I love your grandmother very much. And I know one day you will find a wonderful girl that you will want to spend your life with. You need to be a gentleman to all girls. There are things that you don't do with a girl unless you are married, and I just want you to know of my high expectations for you."

I responded earnestly by saying that I wanted to be a gentleman. I knew this was a one-time conversation — not the kind of thing BD would probably ever talk about again. But I felt uncomfortable because the struggle with desire was already manifesting itself in my thoughts and feelings. BD's words pierced through my young heart and established a clear sense of right and wrong. I knew his words were true and I wanted to be faithful, to meet his expectations and approval. What a challenge. What a struggle. To be told at a young age to save passion for such a long time. I wrestled, I stumbled, I failed, but through my personal disappointments I met God and His love, grace and forgiveness. God's desire for me to wait for my wife became a clear, purposeful conviction in my life. I never forgot BD's brief, direct words. And as I grew in my faith, I learned one of the biblical solutions: FLEE TEMPTATION.

A few years ago BD shared with me some verses from Galations 5:22-23. He told me that when he struggled with thoughts that he knew were not pleasing to God, he would imagine himself exhaling the thoughts as he breathed out and in silent prayer ask God, as he inhaled fresh air, to replace those unpleasing thoughts with the fruit of the Spirit: "love, joy, peace, patience, kindness, goodness, faithfulness, gentleness and self-control." BD gave me such a powerful spiritual tool to help shape my thoughts, attitudes and feelings.

Allen Bell, 28

BD is very giving. He's also caring and always thinks of others first. When I was little I went on a picnic in the woods at Montreat. My dad took Lisel across a log, but when I was going to cross, BD said, "No, let me go first and see if it's safe." He had on his Sunday shoes, and he took a few steps, fell in the creek and broke his ankle.

Olivia Morris, 16

When I had to choose a career for school and do an interview with someone in that field, I chose architecture. I interviewed an architect, but I also decided to interview BD, who had built a lot of office buildings. He told me all about building codes and materials that had to be hurricane proof for offices in Miami. When we finished with that subject, he taught me how to read the stock market reports. He also explained some of the basics about stocks so that I could understand it. Then he said, "Lisel, whatever you choose to do, I know you'll be the best at it. You are so talented, and you need to use each of your gifts to the maximum."

Lisel Morris, 14

What I remember most about BD is the way he always asked me about my favorite things — the Atlanta Braves and my baseball team. Whenever there was a game, he'd turn on the TV and say, "Let's watch the Braves together!" Then he would ask me about my baseball team and he would say, "Always do your best and have fun in your baseball."

Nathaniel Rupp, 13

I feel pretty lucky to have had BD for a grandfather. Visiting him was like going to see a friend. I remember how, whenever he was excited or liked something, he would say, "Hot dog!"

Benjamin Rupp, 13

On days that I was off from school, I'd go to work with my Dad at his office. I liked to answer the telephone, work on the computer, and help Alice, Dad's assistant. BD would compliment me and tell me that he liked to see me working there and that I was doing a good job.

Mallori Joy Morris, 12

BD told me never to point guns at people — even plastic ones that don't have bullets. He told me this when I was about 3 years old so that I would remember it while I'm growing up.

Spencer Morris, 7

My grandfather bought me my first computer, an Apple II+ in 1980, when I was 13 years old. And BD made the initial loan for me to start my software business, IntelliNet. Not a gift; that would make it too easy. It was a toughly negotiated 24-month loan that I made every payment on as we grew the company.

Two weeks before he died, after an article about IntelliNet appeared in the Atlanta Business Chronicle newspaper, BD and I were able to share an afternoon reflecting on our lives together. We also got a chuckle out of the fact that for the first time, instead of being known as the grandson of Allen Morris, HE was known as the grandfather of Frank Bell. The torch has been passed.

BD left a legacy of himself by sharing his time and his values with me. Much of the philosophy behind and the core values of my life and my business are a direct result of this legacy. And I strongly believe these values, based on Biblical principles, are the reason for our success.

Frank Bell, 32

For additional copies of
Living a Legacy,
contact
The Allen Morris Foundation
100 Brickell Avenue
Miami, Florida   33131

(305) 358-1000